The Satanward View

THE
Satanward View
A STUDY IN PAULINE THEOLOGY

by

James Kallas

WIPF & STOCK · Eugene, Oregon

Wipf and Stock Publishers
199 W 8th Ave, Suite 3
Eugene, OR 97401

The Satanward View
A Study in Pauline Theology
By Kallas, James
Copyright©1966 by Kallas, James
ISBN 13: 978-1-5326-9196-6
Publication date 5/16/2019
Previously published by The Westminster Press, 1966

Scripture quotations from the Revised Standard Version of the Bible are copyright, 1946 and 1952, by the Division of Christian Education of the National Council of Churches, and are used by permission.

Acknowledgment is made to Adam & Charles Black, Ltd., London (1953), and The Macmillan Company, New York (1955), for quotations from *The Mysticism of Paul the Apostle,* by Albert Schweitzer.

Dedicated to . . .

... the first generation of California Lutheran College students whose incisive questions sharpened the contents of these pages.

... those pastors of the Lutheran Church in America who were the first to hear these thoughts in just this form, Pacific Lutheran Theological Seminary, Berkeley, California, July, 1964.

... Orville Dahl, for encouragement to write.

CONTENTS

Preface		9
Chapter 1	JESUS AND PAUL	11
Chapter 2	THE GODWARD AND SATANWARD VIEWS	24
Chapter 3	PAUL'S CONVERSION AND CONSEQUENT MISSIONARY LABORS	34
Chapter 4	PAUL'S VIEW OF SIN AND MAN	53
Chapter 5	PAUL'S VIEW OF THE CHURCH, THE NEW CREATION, AND SALVATION	73
Chapter 6	PAUL'S VIEW OF THE BODY OF CHRIST, BAPTISM, AND THE HOLY SPIRIT	92
Chapter 7	CHRISTOLOGY, THE DELAY OF THE END	115
Chapter 8	A STUDY IN DEMYTHOLOGIZING	133

PREFACE

Gustav Aulén is barely mentioned here, and in at least one place Albert Schweitzer is emphatically rejected. However, the perceptive student of the New Testament will see immediately my enormous debt to these two scholars. I have deliberately not quoted from them as often as I should have or could have, simply because, even though I have taken their material, I have taken those materials off into another direction from which Aulén and Schweitzer have gone, and thus to quote from them at length would tend to identify them with a position for which I alone must be responsible.

I have written what I would call "descriptive" theology, as differentiated from what could be termed "applied" theology. That is, my primary attempt has been to show what the motifs and concepts of the New Testament meant *to those people then,* rather than to seek to show what they might mean to us today. Only rarely, and only in passing, have I tried to "apply." Put another way, my main attempt has not been to apply these truths to our time. Indeed, I am often cognizant of the fact that I cannot! I am uncomfortable with many of the conclusions that have been forced on me by these studies. My purpose, then, is not to argue for the relevancy of these motifs as much as it is to point out the danger we face if we fail to reckon seriously with the obvious intent of some very obvious New Testament language. To reject it is to weaken the whole Christian expression. This argumentation is confined pretty much to the final chapter, even as the argumentation over a specific passage or verse is pretty much confined to the footnotes. This has been done in order that my own central positive argument might emerge uncluttered.

To emphasize the other word, this has been written as descriptive "theology." That is, this is not a historical or a literary study, but a theological one. Hence many related, vital questions, even though related and vital (such as the chronology of Paul's life; or the authenticity of his epistles — especially Ephesians; or the literary character of a specific epistle, such as II Corinthians; or the historical difficulty of north or south Galatia), have been flatly ignored and my conclusions on these matters simply presented without supporting evidence. To have pursued them here would have been to lead us away from the primary considerations, and thus the reader is requested to believe that I am at least aware of the problem involved in many of these instances, even if the answer given appears overly facile.

My debt to Charles Kingsley Barrett, of Durham University, England, for counsel, encouragement, and advice, remains enormous.

J. K.

California Lutheran College
Thousand Oaks, California

CHAPTER 1

Jesus and Paul

IN ANY serious study of Paul the question has to be faced, What is his relationship to Jesus? Do their messages agree or conflict? Is Paul what he claims to be, "a slave of Christ" carrying on the message of the risen Lord? Or is he an innovator, an inventor, who has twisted into misshapen forms the simple ethical message of Jesus, thus manufacturing a vast cosmological system of salvation? What is the relationship between Jesus and Paul? This is where one must begin in studying Paul. What is the source of his religion? Did he build on the ministry of Jesus or simply use that ministry as a pretext for his own original creation?

The answers to these questions are of fundamental importance. Paul was the greatest figure of early Christianity outside of Jesus himself. There are twenty-seven books in the New Testament, and at one time or another a full fourteen of them — over half — were ascribed to Paul. It was Paul who made the first recorded missionary journey into Europe. It was Paul who fought the theological battle that freed the church from its nagging bondage to Jewish ritual. By every standard of evaluation — literary, geographical, theological — Paul was the towering figure of the early church, second only to Jesus. This is why every great theological reform movement has based itself on the Pauline epistles. Augustine was a Pauline scholar, and it was from Paul that

Augustine learned the great concept of grace alone. Luther was reading Romans, he tells us, when he suddenly saw the heavens opening and heard the angels singing — and he eventually called another Pauline epistle, Galatians, "my Katie," after his wife. Wesley, though to a lesser degree, was also a Pauline scholar. And in our own time the greatest theological jolt of the twentieth century came in 1917 when Karl Barth's monumental Commentary on Romans first appeared. Paul is the towering theological figure who has influenced the major currents of all theological thought, from New Testament times down to our own.

But, to move on, although all scholars agree that Paul has had an enormous effect on all Christian thought, not all scholars agree that this effect has been beneficial. There has always been a very strong and vocal minority within the Christian family which insists that Paul was a perverter, not a proclaimer, and that instead of transmitting the religion of Jesus, Paul poisoned it. Ernest Renan includes in his evaluation of Paul these words: Paul was an "ugly little Jew. . . . The writings of Paul have been a peril and a stumbling block, the cause of the principal defects of Christianity."[1] What Renan meant by "the principal defects" is perhaps even more clearly seen in the work of the greatest scholar at the turn of the century, Adolf von Harnack. In his massive and impressive work *What Is Christianity?* Harnack's basic thesis was very simple. At the risk of oversimplifying it, what he said in effect was this: Jesus was a fine human being, an outstanding religious teacher who preached an ethical code of the Fatherhood of God and the brotherhood of man. Harnack argued that there was nothing eschatological or cosmological or soteriological in Jesus' message. He taught, not of heaven, but of earth, telling men how to live here and now. Jesus, for Harnack, was not essentially Savior, but rather, good example and fine teacher, who both

---

[1] Quoted by A. M. Hunter, *Interpreting Paul's Gospel* (The Westminster Press, 1955), p. 13.

Jesus and Paul

told men how to live and showed them by precept what he meant. This simple message of Jesus, an ethical code designed to show men the good life here and now, was then taken up and twisted into a mysterious system of otherworldly salvation. The message of Jesus, concentrating on the good life and how to achieve it right now, was perverted into a redemptive cosmological system of release from the devil and eventual salvation through the cross of Jesus. And, in this twisting process, Paul was at least one of the earliest, if not the greatest, of villains. Harnack says substantially the same thing as Renan — that Paul, instead of simply showing Jesus as model to follow and preacher of the brotherhood of men, changed the whole message into something that it was never intended to be.

Now this point of view, although subdued in our time, is nonetheless far from dead. The greatest name in contemporary New Testament theology today, for better or for worse, is Rudolf Bultmann. And Bultmann begins on the same assumption as Renan and Harnack. That is, he begins his discussion of Paul's theology by assuming that the message of Paul is not based upon the work of Jesus, but is instead an entirely new creation rooted, not in the words of Jesus, but in the mind of Paul. Bultmann is not as obvious or as brutal as Renan, but his point of view is unmistakable: "But of decisive importance in this connection is the fact that Paul's theology proper, with its theological, anthropological, and soteriological ideas, is not at all a recapitulation of Jesus' own preaching nor a further development of it. . . . In relation to the preaching of Jesus, the theology of Paul is a new structure." [2]

This, then, in a simplified way, is a constantly repeated view of some of the greatest of New Testament scholars — the insistence that in passing from Jesus to Paul something has changed,

[2] Rudolf Bultmann, *Theology of the New Testament* (London: SCM Press, Ltd., 1956), Vol. I, p. 189.

the message has been twisted, Paul has altered and perverted the simple message of Jesus. Now at least at first glance, there appears to be some Biblical evidence. And that leads me into a very brief review of my earlier monograph on the Synoptic miracles.[3] In Chapter One, I outlined the basic message of Jesus. The first words of Jesus recorded in Mark, ch. 1:14-15, revolved around "the kingdom of God." He says, "The time is fulfilled, and the kingdom of God is at hand." Matthew 4:17-23 and Luke 4:43 (the parallels) agree with Mark. Hence the Synoptics are united in insisting that the opening chord that Jesus strikes concerns the imminent Kingdom of God. The great sermon of Jesus has as its first words a reference to the Kingdom (Matt. 5:3), and once Jesus introduces the theme of the Kingdom in the sermon, he never departs from it (vs. 10, 19-20; later on, the Lord's Prayer, embedded in the sermon, refers to the Kingdom, ch. 6:10; and still the sermon has not finished with references to the Kingdom, ch. 7:21). But Matthew's Jesus did not only preach this one long sermon — he also taught in parables. And the parables too are impregnated with references to the Kingdom. In the discussion of ch. 13:10-12, Jesus insists that the parables have as their purpose the illuminating of certain secrets of the Kingdom, and to make sure the point is not missed, every single parable that follows (and there are seven of them) begins with a direct reference to the Kingdom: "The kingdom of heaven is like unto . . ." (vs. 24, 31, 33, 44, etc.).

It is no overstatement, then, to say that the whole of Jesus' message, his opening words, his great sermon, and his many parables, all revolve around the basic theme of the Kingdom of God. And this motif continues with Jesus right to the end of his life. When he is with his disciples on the night in which he is betrayed, the night of the Last Supper, his thoughts again focus on the

[3] James Kallas, *The Significance of the Synoptic Miracles* (London: S.P.C.K., 1961).

Jesus and Paul

Kingdom (Mark 14:25). At the beginning, middle, and end of his life, his thoughts all shoot inward like converging arrows to the one central fact of the coming Kingdom of God. But, it must be further noticed, this is not simply Jesus' own message. It is also the message that he commissioned his disciples to preach (Matt. 10:5-7; Luke 10:1-9).

This, then, is the first major point: that the entire ministry of Jesus is concerned with one essential point, the Kingdom of God. But whereas this is the dominant, overwhelming, and perhaps even sole consideration of Jesus, when one moves into the epistles of Paul, one appears to have entered a foreign and different atmosphere. This one motif, so vitally central to Jesus, is practically nonexistent in the Pauline letters. And when Paul, rarely, does mention the Kingdom, even the novice Bible reader can see that he speaks of it in a different way. In short, that which was for Jesus central and formative appears to be for Paul peripheral and secondary, relatively minor and unimportant. These are facts, and there are no easy ways around these facts, and it is a battery of facts similar to this that makes scholars such as Renan, Harnack, and Bultmann insist that the theology of Paul is an entirely new creation.

This is a major difference between Jesus and Paul — the very heart of Jesus' message seems to have been set aside by Paul. But, although major, it is not the sole difference. Others may be mentioned. For example, Jesus performed many miracles. As a matter of statistical fact, over 50 percent of the first ten chapters of the Gospel of Mark deals directly or indirectly with the miraculous. But on the other hand, apart from a few references in the Acts, there are no miracles in the ministry of Paul. This fact is important, for it has been interpreted to mean that Jesus performed miracles because he was concerned about this life here and now, freeing man in the immediate moment for a rich life. That is, Jesus was not concerned with " pie in the sky by and by," but was instead concerned with human existence right here in this world. Thus he spent the bulk of his time improving the immediate scene and making it a better place in which to live rather than concerning himself with far-distant heavenly horizons. But Paul, on the other hand, it is maintained, was not concerned with the immediate scene, but with heaven and how to arrive there. In I Cor. 7:21 he seems to condone slavery, telling those who are slaves, " Never mind! " — that is, " Pay it no heed; forget it! " The same point, only even more forcibly made, grows out of the brief note to Philemon in which Paul's action of pleading for the forgiveness of a runaway slave rather than scolding the Christian slaveowner seems to imply an approval of the institution. There is no great social agitation in Paul, no attempt to re-create the immediate scene. Unlike Jesus, Paul is not absorbed in straightening out this world, but is instead absorbed with the next world, salvation in the future.

In line with this, notice well that whereas Jesus stresses right ethical activity here and now (turn the other cheek, render good for evil, give your cloak, go the second mile), Paul instead seems to be concerned, not with good deeds, but with right faith. Paul again and again insists that faith is central, and, even more than that, that faith in the cross of Jesus Christ, where forgiveness of sins is to be found, is central (Rom. 10:9; I Cor. 1:22-24; 15:3). And all this despite the fact that there is not one single place in the Synoptic Gospels where Jesus unambiguously links together his death on the cross and the forgiveness of man's sins, and never does he summon men to believe in that death in the Pauline sense.

But a longer look must be taken at these differences in order to see whether they will bear the weight put upon them. Let us return to the phrase "the Kingdom of God." I have already pointed out, in Chapter Two of my earlier work on the Synoptic miracles, that there were two concepts of the Kingdom that were very much alive in Jesus' day. One concept I called the Davidic

Jesus and Paul

hope — a hope for a kingdom of this world like David's, a political empire, a time when the Jews would rule over all their traditional enemies, the pinnacle of political power. But secondly, there was a Danielic hope that saw the Kingdom as supernatural — not as the climax of Jewish history, but as the end of all history, a heavenly place, a new heaven and a new earth. I also pointed out, in Chapter Three, that whereas the man in the street looked for a Davidic empire in which the Jew would be freed of the Roman, Jesus, on the contrary, was speaking of the Danielic hope, an otherworldly kingdom, a cleansed cosmos. That is the drama of the Synoptic story. The crowds looked to Jesus for one thing, and he intended another. Looking for an earthly kingdom, they went berserk on Palm Sunday, crying out: "Hosanna! Blessed is he who comes in the name of the Lord!" They looked for Jesus to free them from Caesar. But then, later on in the week, they listened in stunned disbelief as he renounced their aspirations and affirmed that his Kingdom was not of this world. And stung by this disappointment, the same lips that had cheered him now curled back in rage and hoarsely cried out: "Crucify him! Crucify him!"

In short, there was this possibility of misunderstanding what Jesus really meant by his phrase "the kingdom of God." He was speaking of a new world cleansed of evil powers, a new world where Satan would be destroyed and the whole world re-created.[4] But the people were looking for a terrestrial military empire of this world. Now, to take a step forward, if there was a possibility for Jesus to be misunderstood, there was an even greater possibility for Paul to be misunderstood. That is, Jesus spoke to a Jewish audience. They were familiar with Daniel and the other

[4] It is precisely this which we have insisted to be the real thrust of his many miracles (see especially Kallas, *op. cit.*, Ch. Six). From this alone we see that those scholars who insist that there was nothing redemptive or cosmological in Jesus' message, seeing it only as a series of ethical axioms, have not rightly grasped his message.

apocalyptic books, familiar with that body of literature which yearned for a cleansed cosmos. That was their heritage and still they misunderstood. Now, if Jews misunderstood, despite their heritage, how much more easily would the Gentile or Greek, not acquainted with that bundle of apocalyptic thought, misunderstand when he heard the phrase "the kingdom of God"? What would the ordinary Greek think when he heard a preacher proclaiming the Kingdom of God? Would he not immediately think of a kingdom here and now? the end of Roman rule and the establishment of a new earthly kingdom with the Christ, rather than Caesar, as it head?

That is exactly what happened. In Acts 17:1-4, we read of Paul at Thessalonica preaching to a Gentile audience. And it appears that Paul actually tried to use the very same words of Jesus, explicitly speaking of a kingdom of God and proclaiming Jesus as king. But what did the hearers conclude? They concluded that Paul was preaching revolution, arguing for revolt, arguing that Jesus and not Caesar was the real ruler: "They are all acting against the decrees of Caesar, saying that there is another king, Jesus." Now an experience such as this convinced Paul that he absolutely could not, under any circumstances, continue to use the same terminology as Jesus. It was open to either gross misunderstanding or willful misconstruction.[5] To preach about the Kingdom of God in a Roman settlement was to lay himself open to the charge of being a dangerous political fanatic arguing for the overthrow of Rome. It is for this reason that Paul laid aside the words of Jesus about the Kingdom of God and introduced an entirely new vocabulary. Paul, in his epistles, does not speak about the Kingdom of God. Instead he speaks about salvation.

[5] A phrase that I have borrowed from W. L. Knox, *St. Paul and the Church of Jerusalem* (Cambridge: Cambridge University Press, 1925), p. 262. W. D. Davies, *Paul and Rabbinic Judaism* (London: S.P.C.K., 1955), p. 37, and J. Klausner, *From Jesus to Paul* (London: George Allen & Unwin, Ltd., 1939), p. 299, also arrive at this same conclusion.

Jesus and Paul

Indeed, salvation and its synonyms are absolutely central and determinative concepts.[6] But it is my contention here that despite the different words that Paul used, he meant exactly the same thing with his vocabulary that Jesus meant with his. What Jesus tried to describe with language about the Danielic kingdom, Paul was seeking to communicate with language about salvation. Paul would have used identical terminology — indeed, tried to — except that it was open to gross misunderstanding, and thus he set aside the literal vocabulary of these words of Jesus. The different vocabularly is due to the fact that Jesus spoke to one audience and Paul to another. Jesus spoke to Jews who ought to have known what the Kingdom meant. Paul, speaking to Gentiles who did not have apocalyptic as their heritage, had to say the same things in other ways.

There is a difference in audience and, therefore, vocabulary, but none in intent. Hence, those scholars who insist, on this basis, that Paul perverted the message of Jesus are not dealing fairly with the facts.

One could go on to note other differences. The fact that Jesus spoke to Jews, to rural Jews, living around the Sea of Galilee in rural Palestine, also determined his imagery and examples. Jesus was a rural man and he spoke of rural things. The birds of the air, the flowers of the field, the sower who went forth to sow, the tares growing with the grain. Jesus was a Jew and quoted Old Testament passages. But Paul was a big-city man, talking to Greeks with a commercial cast to their thought. Thus he spoke

[6] In *The Epistle to the Romans* (London: Adam & Charles Black, Ltd., 1957), p. 27, C. K. Barrett writes: "Paul's argument turns upon salvation. The word itself, even when the cognate verb 'to save' is included in the reckoning, is not one of the commonest in Paul but it is certainly central in his thought." C. A. Anderson Scott says substantially the same thing in *Christianity According to St. Paul* (Cambridge: Cambridge University Press, 1937), p. vii of his preface: "The conception of salvation provides both a centre and a framework for all the religious and ethical ideas which have real importance in Christianity as St. Paul understood it."

of gymnasiums; he spoke of athletic contests known in the Greek world; he used the imagery of the lawcourt and the commercial terms of the big-city marketplace. He quoted Greek pagan poets. But these differences also are due to the difference in audience, and are not due to any perverting or twisting intentions of Paul.

The very minds of these two men, Jesus and Paul, worked in opposite directions. For example, the mind of Jesus always went from an abstract issue to a concrete thought. The favorite teaching device of Jesus was a parable, and that is highly significant, for it shows how his mind worked. He would take an abstract thought about the Kingdom of God and put it into concrete terms, comparing it to a harvest in a field or to a king giving a banquet. Jesus moved from the *abstract* to the *concrete*. But the mind of Paul went in the opposite direction, moving from *concrete* to *abstract*.[7] A specific incident at Corinth, the church divided into factions and cliques, would lead Paul into an abstract discussion of the nature of the church as the indivisible body of Christ.

There are these differences: differences in vocabulary, in imagery, in the sources from which they quote, in the way their minds work.[8] But we would be making a fatal mistake, a foolish

[7] C. A. Anderson Scott has also noticed this characteristic of Paul and writes that there is in Paul's epistles "a digression of a kind characteristic of the Apostle, deducing general precepts from the particular instance" (*op. cit.,* p. 185).

[8] Hence, an approach such as W. D. Davies' (*op. cit.,* pp. 137-143) is dangerous, tending to prove the opposite of what he intends. Davies seeks to show the unity of Jesus and Paul by pointing to those places where Paul actually quotes from the Synoptic tradition (for example, I Cor., ch. 11, the discussion of the Supper). But for every chapter such as I Cor., ch. 11, there are ten other chapters, I Cor., chs. 1 to 10, where Paul does not quote from Jesus' words as they were known. Davies' problem then becomes how to explain the fact that Paul, who knew the words of Jesus well enough to quote them in one place, felt free to ignore those words the majority of the time. The unity of Jesus and Paul is not to be found in the world of words, because, frankly, for the reasons listed, there is little of such unity. Their

mistake, to conclude from these differences that Paul was a perverter rather than a transmitter of that which he had received. Paul, many times in his epistles, considers himself a slave (*doulos*), and argues that "it is no longer I who live, but Christ who lives in me," thus maintaining that he is not the inventor of his own religion but a preacher of the thought of Jesus. It would appear that Renan, Harnack, and Bultmann would make a liar out of Paul on this critical point. Against that view, I must take a stand. Paul is a servant of Christ, captive to his Lord, transmitting that which he has received, not from men, but from God, who revealed himself to Paul in the resurrected Jesus (Gal. 1:1).

The whole basic content of that which follows is based upon that conviction. I would insist that those who see the message of Jesus as basically ethical and Paul as its perverter understand neither Jesus nor Paul. Jesus did not see himself simply as a good example, a fine man showing other well-intentioned men how to live the good life here and now. On the contrary, I have argued in my interpretation of the miracles of Jesus that Jesus saw himself not as model but as Savior, a divine warrior in action, setting men free from the scourges of Satan. This is the way I have explained the miracles, seeing them, not simply as illustrative preaching vehicles embodying a vague general precept about religion, but rather, as a cosmic struggle against Satan. The miracle stories are the history of God in action, seeking to root out and destroy, as Luther would say, "the devil, and all his works, and all his ways." The miracle stories show us Jesus casting out demons and thus demonstrating the superiority of Christ over the demonic element of the world, a direct attack on evil powers. The healing miracles, the nature miracles, the miracles of feeding the multitude, tell us of this same attack, only now an indirect attack, striking not at the demons but rather at the means through

---

unity is to be found in the world of ideas — here they stand together or are separated. Verbal similarities mean very little.

which they work. This same attack is carried to the cross, where Jesus attacks the one great weapon of the devil, death itself, or as the early church put it, "through death he might destroy him who has the power of death, that is, the devil" (Heb. 2:14). The one basic factor tying all these events together, miracles and resurrection, is the idea that God has come to destroy evil forces rampant in the world and to set at liberty the captives who live out their lives under the tyranny of Satan. In such terms Jesus himself summarizes his own work (Mark 3:26-27; Luke 4:18-21).

That, in essence, is the theology of Paul. Paul argues that the cross-resurrection and the return of Jesus at the end of time are great cosmic events. They are the story of Jesus wading into the worst weapon of the devil — death — and emerging victorious, thus assuring the eventual destruction of the cosmic foe and setting men free from their bondage.

In conclusion, it can be seen from what has been said thus far that I maintain that the message of Jesus and Paul is built upon two cornerstones, demonology and eschatology. By demonology, I mean belief in a limited dualism. The New Testament in general and Paul in particular insist that to some degree this world is not under the control of God alone but is under the influence of God's enemy, Satan. Thus I John 5:19 can insist that "the whole world is in the power of the evil one," and twice the Gospel of John can insist that Satan is the "prince of this world" (John 12:31; 16:11). In precisely this strain of thought, Paul can argue that Satan is the "god of this world" (II Cor. 4:4), and can insist that "the *world rulers* of this present darkness" are "the spiritual hosts of wickedness in the heavenly places" (Eph. 6:12). This is why this present time is the present "*evil* age" (Gal. 1:4). This belief in demonology — that this world is a place where Satan is actively causing suffering and death—is the unmistakable thought of Luke 13:16 and it is repeated in Paul in II Cor. 12:7. Further, then, and growing out of this, is the belief

Jesus and Paul

that it is the conviction that this world is under the control of evil forces which produces a hope for the end of the world, eschatology. Jesus looks for the end of the age, the passing away of this heaven and earth (Matt. 24:3, 35). In like manner, Paul is convinced that this present creation is in "bondage to decay" and in the near future "will be set free . . . and obtain . . . glorious liberty" (Rom. 8:21).

These two things, eschatology and demonology, tie Jesus and Paul together. This is what constitutes their oneness. It is not without its own significance that those who reject eschatology-demonology, demythologizing and reinterpreting the message of Jesus in purely subjective terms (Renan, Harnack, Bultmann), can find no real tie between Jesus and Paul, whereas the one man who would insist upon a literal interpretation of eschatology finds a real tie between them.[9] The motif of eschatology-demonology not only welds the life of Jesus into a unity, tying together his precrucifixion acts, the miracles, to his resurrection, seeing them all in the same qualitative light as an attack on Satan. It also ties together Jesus and Paul.

[9] In *Paul and His Interpreters* (London: Adam & Charles Black, Ltd., 1950), p. 160, Albert Schweitzer writes that there is "something in common between the fundamental conceptions of Jesus and Paul on which sufficient stress had not been previously laid." From a different approach and in a different context, Ernest De Witt Burton says the same thing (International Critical Commentary, *Galatians*, p. 431; Edinburgh, T. & T. Clark, 1921): "The two-age eschatology was for Paul not a product of his own thinking, but an inheritance accepted on what he believed to be the authority of Jesus."

CHAPTER 2

The Godward and Satanward Views

SPEAKING BROADLY, there are two ways in which the work of Christ can be grasped. One way is to take seriously the motifs of demonology-eschatology. This view takes seriously the dualism found in the New Testament, which insists that Jesus is come to do battle with the ancient foe of old. In other words, this view develops the work of Christ in terms of conflict. The work of Christ is seen as a joint operation, Father and Son linked together in conflict with evil celestial forces external to the Godhead. The work of Christ is a battle with Satan, aimed at Satan, *Satanward*.

On the other hand, cosmic dualism can be precluded. The literal language of the New Testament can be set aside as mythological, or as an accommodation of language, or as symbolical, but in any event, having no correspondence to metaphysical reality. Satan and the demons can be set aside as the archaic trappings of an antiquated world view no longer acceptable as valid; or else these references to demonic powers can be taken as personifications or concrete depictions of man's own internal impulses and consequent bad acts. In any event, true dualism — a belief in a struggle going on between two cosmic forces outside man, God and Satan — is denied. The work of Christ, then, cannot be outwardly oriented, aimed at an external foe, but must instead be seen as a transaction within the Godhead, between Father and

The Godward and Satanward Views

Son. The object of Christ's work is God. It is unto God that he offers himself as satisfaction for sinful humanity, or it is unto God that he seeks, by means of his own example of obedience, to persuade rebellious man to return. The work of Christ is aimed at God, *Godward*.

Whichever choice a theologian may make, whether that choice be conscious or unreflecting, will have profound implications for every area of his theological development. If cosmic dualism is taken seriously and one ascribes an element of reality to the apocalyptic view that the devil has a measure of real control in this world, certain inevitable conclusions must be drawn concerning the meaning of salvation. Salvation must then be seen as a cosmic or physical act, the cleansing of an enslaved world now subject to an evil head. Eschatology, it follows, must be understood literally as a real end to the world as we now know it. The resurrection and the return of Jesus must be interpreted within the context of victory, a victory in the past at the empty tomb, which is the prelude to the final victory that will take place at the Parousia when Satan's activity will be finally ended. The Kingdom of God, then, by definition, is seen in terms of a liberation of a total world complex at the moment under the hand of Satan. By extension, the suffering that Jesus undergoes must be seen, not as something originating in the will of God, but rather, in the activity of the God-opposing forces. Consequently, suffering in and of itself is not redemptive or cleansing — it has no moral quality to it. It is instead simply the agony of the battlefield, the ordeal through which one must pass on the way to victory — or defeat. If there is no victory, that suffering has no purgative effect, no merit in it. Suffering can be in vain, for the loser as well as the winner of a war suffers.

Conversely, if cosmic dualism is set aside, then one's definition of salvation is altered. In this latter case, salvation is to be seen instead as a present internal or spiritual state affecting the religious attitude of the individual. Salvation then becomes a synonym for reconciliation and forgiveness — not freedom from a foreign foe, but instead, the setting aside of one's own hostility and the pardoning of one's guilt. Here eschatology is seen, not literally as the last hour when Satan will be destroyed, but rather, symbolically as the critical hour in which our rebellion is overcome — not the last hour in time, but the most important hour of decision when a person decides for or against Christ. The Kingdom of God is seen, not as a physical or cosmic entity, a renewed world, but rather, as entry into a right religious relationship with God earlier ruptured by hostility and consequent guilt. Further, another definition must be given to suffering. In itself it is good, originating in God (it could originate nowhere else, for by definition one has precluded any form of dualism). The suffering of Jesus, then, is not an attack of Satan, but a judgment of God being poured out on the one who stands as the representative of sinful man at the bar of God's justice. In line with this, the postbaptismal suffering of the elect must be seen as in some way a supplement to the work of Christ.[1]

[1] This has been the dilemma of Schweitzer. He seeks to interpret the work of Jesus in terms of thoroughgoing eschatology, basing that interpretation upon the apocalyptic books that first produced eschatology. He clearly recognizes that that literature reversed the Old Testament principle of retribution (the belief that suffering originated in God, a punishment for the evil, and that blessing originated in God, a reward for the good) and came instead to insist that suffering was not a work of God, but rather, of the God-opposing forces. Schweitzer acknowledges this alteration in the following passage (*The Mysticism of Paul the Apostle*, tr. from the German by William Montgomery [2d ed., London: Adam & Charles Black, Ltd., 1953; New York: The Macmillan Company, 1955], p. 81): "Whereas the prophets hold that the final tribulation proceeds from God, . . . with Daniel the tribulation is the work of the God-opposing forces." But rather than taking this view seriously, Schweitzer abandons this apocalyptic view and returns to the view that the final tribulation originates in God. It is this view which dominates his interpretation of Jesus going to die. He sees the suffering of the cross as Jesus' submission to the judgment of God. He has a mechanical view — so much suffering must be absorbed in order to satisfy God's judgment. Jesus suffers, but still

The Godward and Satanward Views

The resurrection, from the Godward view, can no longer be seen as a victory, but must instead be seen within the light of a transaction within the Godhead, a sign of God's approval of or acceptance of the work of Christ, already completed in his suffering on the cross. Indeed, in the Satanward point of view, it is the resurrection that is vital, central, the place of triumph over Satan. But in the Godward view the emphasis moves from the resurrection, which is merely a corroborative sign, to the crucifixion itself.[2] It is the cross that becomes central in the Godward view, the place where expiation is made for guilt and where true obedience, the lack of rebellion, is to be seen.

---

the end does not come. Hence, the only conclusion available to Schweitzer is that the suffering of Jesus was insufficient, and that further suffering is demanded. Schweitzer solves this problem by concluding that "fellowship with Christ in suffering and death is the solution of post-baptismal sins. . . . The atoning death of Christ does not procure continuous forgiveness of sins, but only the release obtained in baptism from previously committed sins. For subsequent transgressions atonement is secured by suffering with Christ" (*Mysticism*, pp. 146–147). Schweitzer is simultaneously ascribing a positive purgative aspect to suffering and labeling the work of Christ as insufficient, in need of individual supplement (a point of view that brings him into direct opposition with Paul; see below, pp. 110, 124–126).

[2] This point of view can be well illustrated by referring to the work of James Denney. He flatly rejects demonology and in discussing a passage such as Eph. 6:12, he sarcastically affirms that "such ideas floated before the apostle's imagination" but goes on to insist that such concepts had no formative pertinence for the apostle's thought (*The Death of Christ*, p. 197; London: Hodder & Stoughton, Ltd., 1902). In *Satan, A Portrait* (London: Skeffington & Son, Ltd., 1945), p. 113, Edward Langton also remarks on the total rejection of Satan by Denney: "Dr. Denney, in his notable books *Studies in Theology* and *Jesus and the Gospel*, finds no place for an exposition of the belief in Satan. Of necessity reference is sometimes made to Satan in dealing with passages from the New Testament, but in no single paragraph does the writer deal with the question of Satan's existence and activities." This rejection of demonology demands that Denney move the stress from the resurrection, where Paul places it (I Cor. 15:14, 17), back to the crucifixion. Hence, Denney not only entitles his book *The Death of Christ* but goes on to affirm consistently that "in Romans as in Galatians this death of Christ is the source of all that is Christian" (p. 164),

One's view of sin is also spelled out. From the Satanward view, sin must be seen, not as an act of man, but rather, as a condition of man — man enslaved by forces too potent for him to resist successfully. But this also spells out one's view of man. Man is by definition not self-determining but helpless, exposed to the interference of supernatural powers outside of him that can enter into him even against his will and seize control of him. This has implications not only for one's doctrine of Satan but also for one's doctrine of the Holy Spirit, for they are both grounded in the same basic comprehension of man as open to the interference of external powers, and thus the motif of predestination assumes real significance.

However, within the Godward view, sin is seen, not as a compulsive force holding man enslaved, but as a wrong and perverse abuse of man's freedom — his refusal to bow before his Creator. Thus, here too, man's status is spelled out. Man is by definition free and responsible, and his sin is that he has misused that freedom. A concept of predestination must be rejected, for it is an intrusion upon man's determinative powers.[3]

The choice of either the Satanward or the Godward view determines not only one's view of man and of sin but of the person of Christ as well. The Satanward view would tend to stress the

---

and "His death is in some sense the center and consummation of His work" (p. 9), and "The death of Christ and its significance was not St. Paul's theology, it was his gospel. It was all that he had to preach!" (p. 109). The facts will not bear this evaluation. See below, pp. 76–78.

[3] C. H. Dodd rejects the view of man as helpless: "We note this as against the doctrine of 'total depravity' and the complete impotence of the human will which have been ascribed to Paul" (*The Epistle to the Romans*, p. 37; London: Hodder & Stoughton, Ltd., 1954). He rejects demonology, insisting upon the "divineness of the natural order" (*The Parables of the Kingdom*, p. 22; London: James Nisbet & Co., Ltd., 1953), and rejects Paul's cosmological observations on Rom. 8:21 f. as a "pessimistic mood. . . . Paul has made of this a truly poetical conception as little as possible dependent on any particular metaphysics" (*The Epistle to the Romans*, pp. 133–134). He has rejected eschatology: "These future tenses are only an accommodation of language. There is no coming of the

The Godward and Satanward Views

divinity of Jesus, his oneness with the Father, the two locked together in combat with the devil. His obedience is active execution of the Father's will. The Satanward view revolves around the celestial aspect of Jesus, for only one who is divine would be able to meet so potent a foe on anywhere near equal grounds. But if there is no demonic tyrant to be bested, the stress is automatically on the humanity of Jesus — the emphasis is not on the unity of the Father and Son but on the subordination of Son to Father.[4] Jesus' life is offered up to God as Jesus the perfect man offers his own sinless life in the place of sinful humanity. Here the obedience of Jesus is seen, not as active execution, but as pas-

---

Son of Man 'after' His coming in Galilee" (*The Parables of the Kingdom*, p. 108). Hence, predictably, having rejected demonology-eschatology and seeing man as self-determinative, he must flatly reject the whole Pauline emphasis upon predestination, insisting that the discussion of that motif in Rom., chs. 9 to 11, is "the weakest point in the whole epistle" (*The Epistle to the Romans*, p. 159).

[4] This is Vincent Taylor's problem. He just assumes that the work of Jesus is exclusively Godward. Thus he can entitle a book *Forgiveness and Reconciliation* (subjective or internal personal effects of Christ's work) and make no references in that title to *salvation* (the objective release from external forces, the key word in Pauline vocabulary, see above, Ch. 1, n. 6). Working within a Godward frame of reference, he defines sin (*in the Preface of his work*, as an a priori assumption, giving no Biblical evidence for the conclusion) as an act of man, rebellion and consequent guilt: "As a state, sin is a condition of alienation from God, not merely one of ignorance, although ignorance is an important conditioning factor, but of hostility towards Him and His purpose. As expressed in action, sin is self-regarding activity; it is the assertion of selfish interests in opposition to the love and will of God. . . . Sin is egoistic and destructive of fellowship with God and men" (*Forgiveness and Reconciliation*, pp. xix–xxi; London: Macmillan & Co., Ltd., 1941). Having begun in this exclusively Godward context, Taylor predictably affirms God as the controller of the cosmos and the source of this world's suffering, suffering being seen as a positive purgative force: "The Creator . . . has set man in a world of trial, in which exposure to evil and the possibility of sin are essential to growth in freedom and sonship" (*The Atonement in New Testament Teaching*, p. 284; London: The Epworth Press, 1940). Having made these statements, seeing God as in control and suffering as a purgative factor, Taylor recognizes that an exclusively Godward interpretation tends

sive submission to the will of the Father working on him.

One could extend this discussion indefinitely, going through such terms as the Sacraments, faith, sanctification, ethics, etc., but enough has been said to make clear the fact that the Godward and Satanward views do not differ simply in detail or degree, but they are instead fundamentally different comprehensions of the whole spectrum of theological thought. In sketchy tabular form the two views would appear like this:

	SATANWARD	GODWARD
Jesus		
His nature	Divine	Human
Type of person	Liberator, or Savior	Model, or Good Example
His obedience	Active	Passive
His crucifixion	Attack by Satan	Judgment of God
His resurrection	Victory over Satan	Corroborative sign
His return	Final destruction of Satan	Symbolically, not literally seen

to pit the loving Son against the harsh justice of the demanding Father. Taylor sees that the dualism he has refused to recognize outside of the Godhead is consequently thrust into the Godhead, and Father and Son are separated. Thus he writes: "There is the difficulty of apprehending how the Atonement as the purpose of God is fulfilled in the work of Christ . . . without dividing the unity of the Godhead by setting the representative ministry of the Son over against the love, justice and mercy of God." (*Atonement*, p. 268.) Not only here but elsewhere (for example, *Atonement*, pp. 306–310), Taylor finds himself obliged to reaffirm the unity of the Godhead, for he recognizes that his exclusively Godward interpretation threatens that unity; thus he must disavow the obvious conclusion growing out of his statements. The Godward view *does* subordinate Jesus to the Father. Significantly, Taylor, just like Schweitzer (see note 1 of this chapter), is forced into considering the work of Christ as insufficient and needing a supplement supplied by the suffering Christian: "Unique as His [Jesus'] thought of Messianic suffering was, He nonetheless regarded it as a redemptive activity which, in their own measure, men were to reproduce in their own lives" (*Atonement*, p. 21).

The Godward and Satanward Views

	SATANWARD	GODWARD
Sin		
Its nature	Enslaving power	Rebellion and consequent guilt
Nature of man	Helpless, open to external powers	Free, self-determining
Salvation (Kingdom of God)		
When	Future	Now
Its nature	Objective, cosmic in scope	Subjective, internal religious experience
Man's entry	Predestination	Personal decision
This world		
Its ruler	Satan	God
Source of suffering	Satan	God
Nature of suffering	Evil, nonredemptive, work of Satan	Good, purgative act of God

The chart, like the preceding discussion, could be continued indefinitely, but that serves no further purpose. It remains to draw some conclusions. First, the good Bible student immediately recognizes that there is abundant Scriptural evidence for both views. The most obvious example is that the Christian community does not choose between either the humanity or the divinity of Jesus, but insists upon both. Or, to take another example, Luke 13:16 definitely sees suffering as an attack of Satan, whereas Heb. 12:3 ff. sees it as a chastisement of a loving Father. In Paul, to move to another example, man is at one point called free and responsible, without excuse for his actions (Rom. 2:1), and in another place he is called helpless (ch. 7:15 f.). Predestination is such a real thought to Paul that it is not only emphatically affirmed in isolated passages (Phil. 1:29; Rom. 8:29), but it is also the subject of a discussion several chapters long (Rom., chs. 9 to 11); yet side by side with that, there are the oft-repeated imperatives of the epistles and the exhortations of the Synoptics, " Come unto me. . . ."

This, then, is the very first observation to be drawn — both views can be bulwarked at every step by Scriptural evidence. Secondly, then, and growing out of this, is the insistence that Biblical truth is found, not in one column or in the other, not by choosing, but by holding both in tension. The Hebrew tendency to dialectic, so repugnant to the logical Greek mind, must be accepted, and opposites held together. When the two are separated, it is not that one has half the truth, but that one has no truth, for truth sundered from opposite but equally valid counter truth becomes not truth but distortion. To separate the two motifs is to shatter them. The work of Christ is rightly understood only by holding these two opposing views in tension, for in the deepest sense they are not contradictory, but complementary.

This will be the basic attempt in the pages that follow — to insist that both the Godward and Satanward views are valid. Further, I will insist that when one or the other of these motifs is ignored or rejected, the result is something less than the full, rich, varied comprehension of Jesus put forth by the Gospel writers.

However, I shall also seek to assert that whereas both of these views are valid, nonetheless one is primary and determinative, and the other is secondary and derivative. I have already insisted, in the interpretation I gave of the miracles, that the Satanward view is the fundamental view of the Synoptics, and I shall go on to insist that it is precisely this view which dominates Paul. Translated into mathematical terms, although both views are valid, the Satanward view comprises about 80 percent of Paul and of the Synoptics, and the Godward view about 20 percent.

The Godward and Satanward Views

It is my further view (although this negative aspect will not be emphasized until the last chapter) that it is precisely this fact — the dominance of the Satanward view — which contemporary theology has not accepted. Rather than acknowledging the formative nature of this motif, contemporary theology has interpreted the work of Jesus in primarily, if not exclusively, Godward terms. The end result is that much of that which calls itself New Testament theology today is not a characterization of Biblical thought but a caricature — the shattered, barely alive half of a mutilated Siamese twin who has survived the vivisection, but only barely. The rejection of the Satanward view has been catastrophic in result, affecting our view of man, of sin, of the world, of the nature and work of Jesus. All these have borne the scars of the loss of the Satanward view.

CHAPTER 3

Paul's Conversion and Consequent Missionary Labors

IN THIS CHAPTER we shall discuss, not Paul's theology proper, but two earlier events of his life which will help us to grasp his theology when we address ourselves to it directly. We look first at his conversion and later at his missionary experiences.

First, let us glance at the approximate chronology of his life, for that chronology will have significance, especially for the second topic of discussion in this chapter.

APPROXIMATE CHRONOLOGY OF PAUL'S LIFE

1. Ascension of Jesus, A.D. 29.
2. Paul's conversion, A.D. 33.
3. Paul's first missionary journey: after the death of Herod, A.D. 44, and before the Council of Jerusalem, A.D. 50. Approximate dates — A.D. 46–48.
4. Paul's second missionary journey: begun in the spring of A.D. 51 (after the Council of Jerusalem, Acts 15:36), at least one year for early events (chs. 15:36 to 17:34), at least one and a half years in Corinth (ch. 18:11). Approximate dates — A.D. 51–53. (First epistles written on this voyage, I and II Thessalonians, both from Corinth.)
5. Paul's third missionary journey: begun in the spring of A.D. 54, three years in Ephesus (Acts 20:31), an eventual

Conversion and Voyages

autumn in Macedonia (v. 2), and winter in Corinth (v. 3), returned to Jerusalem and was imprisoned under Felix (ch. 24:27). Approximate dates — A.D. 54–58. (Epistle to the Galatians written from Ephesus, as were, later, I Corinthians and II Corinthians, chs. 10 to 13, II Corinthians, chs. 1 to 9, written from Macedonia, and Romans written from Corinth.)

6. Accession of Festus as governor (Acts 24:27) and Paul sent to Rome, A.D. 60.
7. Two years in Roman imprisonment (Acts 28:30). Approximate dates — A.D. 61–63, followed by martyrdom. (Epistles to the Colossians, Ephesians, Philippians, and Philemon written from Roman imprisonment.)

We begin with Paul's conversion experience, which is so well known that it needs no rehearsal here. When we first meet him, he is not Paul the apostle, but Saul the persecutor. He himself tells us in his epistles and through the narratives of The Acts that he was from Tarsus, a center of Greek culture. He was also a Roman citizen. Thus he had the background of those two worlds and the advantages of each. But also, and most especially, he was a Jew "of the tribe of Benjamin, a Hebrew born of Hebrews; as to the law a Pharisee, . . . as to righteousness under the law blameless; . . . advanced in Judaism beyond many of my own age among my people, so extremely zealous was I for the traditions of my fathers" (an amalgam of Phil. 3:5-6 and Gal. 1:14). He was a student of Jewish traditions and law under Gamaliel during the days of Jesus, and although we are not at all sure that he ever heard Jesus preach, we know that he eventually encountered the teachings of the followers of Jesus, and that the encounter infuriated him. The earliest Christians, of course, made no effort to disassociate themselves from the Temple because they saw themselves as true Jews. Indeed, the very name "Christian," used to distinguish them, did not come into being for yet another decade. Since they saw themselves as true Jews, they continued to go to and from the Temple. Even more implicit in their convictions was the assumption that not only were they, the followers of Jesus, true Jews, but actually they were the *only* true Jews, for they believed that the hopes and promises of the Old Testament were fulfilled in the Jesus whom they worshiped as Messiah and Lord. Implicit in that assumption was the accusation that those who did not believe in Jesus were not true Jews, having rejected the Jewish Messiah of God.

It does not take much insight to see what kind of effect a claim like that would have on a young "Hebrew of Hebrews, . . . advanced in Judaism, . . . extremely zealous for the traditions of the fathers." Here is Saul, a learned man, spending years of his life in intense study devoted to the glory of Israel, being suddenly told by implication that he is not really a Jew because he does not believe in Jesus. What an affront! What an insult it must have appeared, to be told by unlettered fishermen, ex-prostitutes, and former tax collectors that he was not a Jew because he was not prepared to accept the proposition that the whole of the Old Testament had reached its climax on the day when a carpenter's son from the despised little town of Nazareth had been nailed to the cross — being told that the glorious hope of the Jews had been aimed at this, Roman crucifixion! — and that unless he accepted it, he was disinherited!

It goes without saying that Saul saw this not only as preposterous but as blasphemous, insulting, a diabolical plot of the devil himself designed to ridicule and discredit Jewish hopes. And thus, because of his zeal for God,[1] he became a persecutor of the church ("as to zeal a persecutor of the church," Phil. 3:6). The first time we meet Saul in the New Testament he is organizer

---

[1] The fact that his *zeal* led him to persecute the church is not without its own significance. See below, pp. 110, 124–126.

behind the death of the first Christian martyr, Stephen (Acts 8:1). Even the death of Stephen is not enough for him, so he takes the road to Damascus, vowing to continue there the persecuting work begun in Jerusalem. But he never makes it. The absolutely dramatic story, emotionally moving for anyone who has powers of imagination, is engraved on Christian consciousness. He is knocked to the ground by a blinding light, hears a voice crying out to him, "Saul, Saul, why do you persecute me?" He answers, "Who are you, Lord?" And the voice responds, "I am Jesus, whom you are persecuting." (Acts 9:4-5.) And Saul is a changed man, literally turned inside out, or, as he says, "The old has passed away, behold, the new has come. . . . If any one is in Christ, he is a new creation" (II Cor. 5:17). Life begins anew. The persecutor has become the apostle. Not right away, of course, but the corner is already turned. He is led, blinded, to Damascus, Ananias baptizes him, the blindness disappears, and Saul goes out to preach in the local synagogue, saying of Jesus, "He is the Son of God" (Acts 9:20).

Every scholar who has ever read the life of Paul has to recognize this conversion experience as the crucial event of this man's life. It is impossible to do otherwise, so dramatic is the before and after change of his life. But although all theologians agree on the centrality of this conversion event, the roads of the theologians begin to diverge when they interpret the event. There are two general ways in which the event can be interpreted. One is the subjective interpretation; the other is objective.

Perhaps it is true to say that the overwhelming bulk of scholars today take the subjective view. In effect, what is claimed is something like this: that the event was purely internal, subjective, confined to the mind of Paul, and not to be accepted in a wooden or literal fashion as portrayed in The Acts. If you had been there with camera and sound recorder, the camera would have recorded nothing and no sound would be preserved, for the event took place as a psychological rather than a crassly historical event. As evidence of this view, some facts can be brought forward. For example, it must be recognized that the conversion of Paul is told, not once, but three separate times in The Acts, and in those tellings the details do not agree. This indicates that the story is not to be taken literally but psychologically and that what is in play here is the usual Jewish tendency to describe intangibles with concrete word pictures, in the way that Jesus would tell a parable. (The discrepancies of the three stories, Acts 9:1-19; 22:4-16; and 26:9-18, include such facts as that in ch. 9:7 the men with Paul hear the Voice but see nothing, whereas in ch. 22:9 his companions see the light but hear nothing.)

This deliteralizing of the event is done not to discredit the story but to make it more relevant to us. None of us was ever knocked off a horse, rolled in the dust by a loud voice, and blinded by supernatural forces; hence, the experience of Paul seems remote, not related to normal existence. To make it more relevant, the attempt is made to cast it into a subjective experience, indicating how the experiences of Paul are shared by mankind in general. All of us have gone through the psychological experience of going one way to try to find peace with God, being frustrated, and then finally finding Christ and gaining peace. Looked at from this view, Paul's life has immediate import for the whole Christian family. Here is a man who tried to find peace with God through his own efforts under the law but came to see that he was on the wrong track. There is the uneasy realization, at first ill defined, but growing in intensity, that personal effort is not enough. Fearful and uneasy, he becomes hostile toward that which appears to threaten him, the church. He attacks and murders Stephen. This does not end his fears but only inflames them. He sees this lowly deacon stoned to death, without a word of reproach, praying for his assassins, and Saul is profoundly affected. He sees a man who has so much to live for that he is willing to die for it, sees that Stephen has drunk from deeper wells than he, Saul, has yet tasted. Thus, in this apparent moment of triumph, Saul is already being beaten. He sees that his own life will never give him the courage and the confidence that he has just witnessed. With a mounting sense of dread, frighteningly aware of the fact that he is on the wrong road — kicking against the goads — he sets out for Damascus. In this disturbed and emotional state of mind, he has the conversion experience. In his mind's eye, he suddenly sees in a blinding insight of illumination the actual truth. He knows that he is opposing that which he ought to be embracing. And thus, when he realizes this, he falls prostrate, is led to Damascus, and converses with and is comforted by Ananias. The pieces fall into place, and symbolically the scales fall away. He sees the full truth and is now ready to preach that which he earlier persecuted.

The objective view is much easier to describe. It simply insists that the truth of the event is to be found, not in trying to psychologize this experience, but by taking it literally, objectively, in the form in which The Acts presents it. Here is a man who is a raging enemy at one moment, and at the next moment is flattened by the power of God, which turns him inside out and sets him off in an entirely new direction.

Despite the impressive array of theologians who give a subjective view, Paul's conversion will bear no such weight of psychological interpretation. There are powerful reasons why a subjective view is inadequate. In the first place, one of the key points of the subjective view is the assumption that before his conversion Saul was nagged by unrest or uneasiness, failure to find peace with God under the law.[2] We are asked to believe that before his

[2] Taylor, for example, assumes this, and it is this earlier sense of frustration, stemming from the law's inadequacy, which, according to Taylor, accounts for Paul's later negative attitude to the law: "Paul . . . uses language of the strongest kind about the limitations and temporary character of the law. . . . It is the language of intense spiritual disappoint-

Damascus road experience he was haunted by a sense of failure. This just does not fit the facts. On the contrary, Paul adamantly insists that his preconversion life was never characterized by such a sense of futility. For example, in Phil., ch. 3, Paul discusses his earlier life, and there is not one single word that betrays such an uneasiness. On the contrary, he insists that he was at that time a self-confident, boisterous, vigorous young man who was fully convinced that he was on the right track, not the wrong one, and that in his actions he was fighting for the glory of God. It was his zeal that motivated him, not fear (Phil. 3:6). He was fully assured in his own mind that he was serving God in persecuting those who dared to insult the Jewish faith. The psychological or subjective view, at this key issue, has absolutely no grounding in Paul. As a matter of fact, Paul makes it clear that if there was a time when he felt an internal struggle, the soul divided against itself, it was not before his conversion but after! It is in Rom., ch. 7, that Paul the Christian tells of the war going on within him,

---

ment" (*Atonement*, pp. 113–114). Paul's negative attitude toward the law stems, not from psychological disappointment, but rather, from cosmological considerations. It is his conviction that the law, which was good and sent of God, had capitulated and was under the control of God-opposing forces, numbered with the enemy, hence, not only unnecessary to observe, but downright dangerous to adopt, for it was to "turn back again to the weak and beggarly elemental spirits" (Gal. 4:9) who stood behind the law. Dibelius is closer to Paul than Taylor when he writes in *Paul*, p. 118, that "Paul was quite sure that behind the breakdown of the law he could see the working of sin, and that demonic power of which we have already spoken." Hence, the law being identified with the God-opposing forces, Schweitzer can rightly affirm that the central thrust of Galatians is not Godward, but Satanward, not a transaction between Father and Son, but an attack on demonic powers active in the law. "It should be carefully observed that it is not a question of an atonement made to God through Christ, but of a most skillfully planned foray made by Christ against the angel-powers, by means of which He frees those who are languishing under the law, Gal. 4:5" (*Mysticism*, p. 212). To pursue the topic further here is impossible. It is too large a subject, demanding a monograph, not an extended note.

Conversion and Voyages

of the tug that shreds him and renders him wretched.[8] Paul argues that it is only after he came into the church that his real inner ten-

[8] The obvious answer to this dilemma is to go against the *prima facie* evidence of the verb tenses and assert Rom., ch. 7, to be, not a present experience of Paul the apostle, but a pre-Christian remembrance of how Saul the persecutor had felt. This is the route taken by most theologians. Scott thus tells us that Rom., ch. 7, is a description of a man "prior to or apart from faith-union with Christ" (*op. cit.*, p. 235). W. D. Davies (*op. cit.*, p. 24) insists that Rom., ch. 7, is a reminiscence of Paul's pre-Christian days. In *St. Paul and the Church of the Gentiles* (Cambridge: Cambridge University Press, 1939), p. 98, Wilfred Knox writes: "Romans 7 is an impressive statement of Paul's experience of failure before his conversion." For Arthur D. Nock (*St. Paul*, p. 68; London: Butterworth & Co., Ltd., 1938), Rom., ch. 7, is a "generalized retrospect, a pre-conversion experience." The list can be lengthened by the addition of almost every man who has ever written on Rom., ch. 7. Even Schweitzer insists: "The desperate battle between the inward man and fleshly man, which Paul describes in Romans 7, is therefore not a post-baptismal but a pre-baptismal experience" (*Mysticism*, p. 296). About the only scholars who are willing to accept the text as it stands, seeing Rom., ch. 7, as the verb tenses and context demand that it be seen, a present experience, are C. K. Barrett (*op. cit.*, pp. 151–153) and Anders Nygren (*Commentary on Romans*, pp. 292–293; Muhlenberg Press, 1949). C. H. Dodd, having conceded that the obvious intent of the passage is to indicate a postbaptismal event (*The Epistle to the Romans*, p. 59), resorts to the dubious expediency of seeking to rewrite the text to suit his own theological purposes. Paul, in Rom. 7:25a, breaks out in an exclamation of liberty, but goes on to affirm immediately afterward, in the very same verse, that he nonetheless is still a prisoner of sin. This fits in perfectly with the Satanward view, which we shall go on to develop (see below, pp. 76–78), which claims that man, even after union with Christ, is still exposed to the tyrant Sin. But this does not fit in with Dodd's Godward view, which sees sin exclusively in terms of rebellion of responsible man. Hence, Dodd seeks to alter the order of verses, insisting that Rom., ch. 7, ought to read, as the order of verses, 22, 23, 25b, 24, 25a. And as justification for this, Dodd writes: "The amanuensis got confused. . . . We do seem to have here one of the cases where primary corruption affected all surviving MSS., and we cannot avoid trusting our own judgment against their evidence" (*Romans*, p. 115). This really is impossible exegesis! When Paul talks of the world as enslaved, it is dismissed as a "pessimistic mood" (*Romans*, p. 133), and when Paul talks of cosmic forces warring on man, we are told that "Paul has made of this a truly poetical conception, as little as possible dependent on any particular

sion began. We will discuss this later in depth,[4] but for the moment we simply notice that the assumption of the subjective view — that Paul was emotionally disturbed before conversion — is not verified, but contradicted, by Paul's own language.

Another strong bit of evidence against the subjective view is this: the whole theology of Paul which one finds in his epistles is grounded on the fact that he has seen the risen Lord Jesus Christ. The Judaizers, his enemies at Galatia, and later his own converts at Corinth, accuse him of being an inferior disciple. The Judaizers argue that he is subordinate to the Jerusalem disciples, dependent upon what he has learned from Peter and the others. But in Gal. 1:1, Paul thunders out, "Paul an apostle — not from men nor through man, but through Jesus Christ." Where had he met this Jesus, where had he been commissioned to be an apostle? At the Damascus road experience. If we reduce that event to an internal or psychological experience, the product of a temporarily demented and disturbed mind, we are in effect arguing that the whole later ministry of Paul and the conviction upon which that ministry was based was a hallucination, an imagining and not an objective fact. And *that* is psychologically unsound! It is impossible to believe that Saul could have been one type at his conversion — emotional, unbalanced, tending to instability, besieged by hallucinations — and later the rock of fortitude and courage that he revealed himself to be when he was beaten all across Asia Minor, his back laid bare by the lash of the law, stoned and beaten to near death all through the Anatolian foothills. We cannot build that kind of strength upon the hypothesis of earlier weakness. It contradicts Paul's own clear word that he had literally met the risen Lord and was commissioned by him, as well as defying the rudiments of psychology. Paul was always

---

metaphysics" (*Romans*, p. 134). Finally, when Paul comes out of his pessimistic mood and lays aside his poetry, the amanuensis gets confused!

[4] See below, pp. 82–84.

Conversion and Voyages 43

a strong man — not emotionally erratic, but steady, hard, tough. He was a tough, hard man who was grasped by a force greater than himself, objectively grasped,[5] and, even against his will, sent off in a new direction.

As we conclude this discussion of the conversion, it must be seen that this is no mere theologian's quarrel — objective or subjective. The position adopted here has profound and far-reaching influence on one's whole comprehension of Paul's theology. If one assumes that this was a subjective experience, one has already made key assumptions in respect to the nature of man and the nature of the God-man relationship. One is, in effect, saying that man is the key actor — or at least active. Here is seeking man, going one way in trying to find God, failing, and then going another way in trying to find God, and succeeding. First, seeking God under the law, then seeking God in the church. First, one is saying that man is the responsible actor, able to look, able to decide. And second, one is saying that it is man who establishes the God-man relationship in the final analysis. The picture is Godward, responsible man seeking out God, first failing, and then achieving. In visual terms, the quest is characterized by an upward-slanting arrow depicting man looking for God.

But that is not the view of Paul. For Paul, man is the sought, not the seeker: Gal. 1:15, "He who had set me apart before I was born"; Phil. 1:29, "It has been granted to you that . . . you should . . . believe in him"; [6] Phil. 3:12, "Christ Jesus has made

---

[5] "Christ Jesus has made me his own," Paul says in Phil. 3:12, and the verb *katalambanō* is a very strong one. Johannes Munck, commenting on this passage in *Paul and the Salvation of Mankind* (London: SCM Press, Ltd., 1959), p. 23, insists that the verb means "the forcible seizure of Paul by someone stronger who would not let him go; . . . to seize or overpower."

[6] On this verse, Bultmann writes: "Paul can say that faith in Christ is 'granted' as a gift — Phil. 1:29. In fact, he can speak of it in downright predestinarian terms — Rom. 8:29; 9:6-29" (*op. cit.*, p. 329).

me his own."[7] The actor in Paul's version of Christianity is not man, but God. It is God who seeks and saves, and visually depicted, that is a downward-slanting arrow. In line with this is Paul's whole basic anthropological conviction that man is open to the intervention of supernatural forces that can reach into a man's existence and alter his destiny. Paul's doctrine of the Holy Spirit is based upon this unshakable belief that God can actually reach into a man's life and alter him and put him on a new road. This is precisely why Paul can develop the view of the Sacrament of Baptism that he does, making that act dependent for its efficacy, not upon man, but upon God in action.[8]

The conversion of Paul, then, is to be grasped as an objective event: not the meanderings of a disturbed mind seeking God, but the act of a powerful God plunging anew into this world. There is a view of man here who is exposed to the interference of supernatural forces outside of himself, both good and evil. And this is the Satanward view, the conviction that man is not entirely self-determining. Or, as Luther put it, "man is a beast of burden, made to be ridden, and he cannot always choose his own rider." Thus Luther could go on to write *The Bondage of the Will*. Satan and the Spirit are opposites. Yet in one sense they are identical, for they are part of the same world view of spirits active outside man, part of the same anthropology that sees man as open to such spiritual activity.

We turn now to the missionary journeys of Paul. We can begin by insisting that, unfortunately, we have often romanticized the life of Paul to such an extent that we end up fictionalizing it. We often think of Paul as the persecutor being struck down into the dust and immediately going forth from there aflame for the preaching of the gospel. It is not quite that simple, despite a pas-

[7] We have already commented on the meaning of this verb in note 5 above.
[8] See below, pp. 101–105.

Conversion and Voyages 45

sage such as Acts 9:20. We often think of Paul as a great missionary strategist setting up long-range planning, fired with a vision of the expansion of the gospel, planting the church in a key center from which it could radiate outward, and then quickly hustling on to another center and repeating the same program. We see him as a master planner of the church, working frantically while there was yet day, convinced that the night was coming and that much must be done both before the end came and in order to make the end come.[9] It is not that simple. Such a view of Paul is not factual. It does not fit the record as that record is revealed in the book of The Acts.

In the first place, there are the bare facts of date. Paul was converted about A.D. 33. His first missionary journey did not take place until about A.D. 46–48. Allowing for an error of a few years in dating, and even allowing for a passage of time spent in work at Antioch with Barnabas, we are still confronted by the staggering fact that a minimum of a full decade passed by between his conversion and his first activity within the church! What did he do in those years? As far as we can tell, he did absolutely nothing! We know he went home to Tarsus, where Barnabas later came to seek him. He did not come out of retirement of his own will. Barnabas sought him! (Acts 11:25.) And there is not one single word out of the early traditions of the church that tells us that a church was ever founded there at Tarsus due to Paul's ministrations! As far as known facts are concerned, Paul just sat

---

[9] This is the central thesis of Munck's work *Paul and the Salvation of Mankind*. It is Munck's view that "with Paul it is not a matter of a call to apostleship in general, but of a clearly defined apostleship in relation to the Gentiles" (p. 41). Further, "as long as the gospel has not reached the Gentiles, Christ's return cannot take place" (p. 276). Coupling these two facts together, Munck concludes that "Paul regards himself as the one upon whom the Messianic Age depends. . . . Paul as the apostle to the Gentiles becomes the central figure in the story of salvation" (pp. 41, 49). The argument that follows directs itself against such a view.

there on his hands, his mouth closed, for over a decade. Now this is an astounding fact, and it becomes even more astounding when we read in his first epistles, I and II Thessalonians, that Paul expected the return of Jesus in the immediate future, in his own lifetime, while he was still alive (I Thess. 4:15-17). He believed this return to be so imminent — not a month or a year off, but this afternoon or tomorrow at the latest — that his counsel caused the Thessalonians to give up their jobs and wait for the end to come to rescue them from their idleness.

That, then, is the problem. Paul expected the end to come right away, and despite that fact, he never made any effort to preach the gospel. He simply withdrew, going into retirement at Tarsus. The ordinary thought might be, "The end is close; let us work while there is still time." But such was not the thought of Paul. And indeed, Paul was not the exception. This was the attitude of the earliest church. This becomes quite clear when one reads the early chapters of The Acts. After the ascension, and even after Pentecost, the early church felt no compulsion or obligation to leave Jerusalem and go out and preach. This is why we have stories such as Acts 3:1 f., *after Pentecost,* with Peter and John going to and from the Temple, with no apparent plans to depart from Jerusalem.

Now the reasons behind this behavior are relatively simple. The explanation can be found by returning to the two key words we have already used: eschatology and demonology. In the first place, the people literally believed that the end was very close. Hence, there would be no time for them to begin, much less execute, a gigantic missionary program. Evidences of the expectation of a near return are found throughout Paul's epistles; passages such as I Thess. 4:15-17; I Cor. 7:29, 31; and Rom. 13:11 are only a few examples.[10] This view, of course, traces back to

[10] Schweitzer writes: "From his first letter to his last Paul's thought is always uniformly dominated by the expectation of the immediate return

Jesus himself, who apparently had predicted that the end would come within the lifetime of his hearers (Matt. 10:23; Mark 9:1; 14:62).

Secondly, the people believed in demons. They literally believed that this world was under the heel of celestial evil world rulers (I Cor. 2:8; II Cor. 4:4; Eph. 6:12) against whom they, as ordinary humans, could do nothing. Thus they did nothing.

But they were further convinced that even though they could do nothing, something would be done. It would be done directly by God himself, for only God was strong enough to succeed against such a foe. The early church was fully convinced that a missionary program would be executed and that God would gather his elect. He would accomplish this, not by using ordinary men — they were not strong enough — but would use the angels instead. Again this view traces back to Jesus himself, who explicitly insisted that it would be "*his angels* [who] . . . will gather his elect from the four winds, from one end of heaven to the other" (Matt. 24:31; the Marcan parallel, ch. 13:27, says exactly the same thing).[11]

---

of Jesus." (*Mysticism*, p. 52.) In *Paul* (London: Hodder & Stoughton, Ltd., 1902), pp. 13–14, Adolf Deissmann writes: "His glowing hope never reckoned on coming centuries. . . . The hope that the present age of the world was hastening to its close, and that the new world of the kingdom of God was about to appear dominate his epistles." These statements have never been repudiated, nor even seriously challenged.

[11] This expectation that angels would gather in the elect also accounts for an otherwise insoluble difficulty of the Synoptic account. On the one hand, Jesus can prohibit his disciples from reaching outside the Jews: "Go nowhere . . . but . . . to the lost sheep of the house of Israel" (Matt. 10:5-6); and yet he envisages people coming from east and west to be part of the elect. These are not Jews of the Dispersion, but Gentiles, for it specifically insists that they take the place of the rejected Jews. (Ch. 8:11-12.) The contradiction is seen in that Jesus understood the task of himself and his disciples to reach Israel, and the angels would bring in those from the outside — hence he could prohibit the evangelization of the Gentiles and yet anticipate their presence in the Kingdom.

Thus, it was this world view which accounts for the otherwise incomprehensible failure of the early church in general, including Paul, to act. They believed that they had no time to act, and that even if they had time, they would lack the power to act. Hence, it must be God who would act directly. In the meantime, Peter and John could go to the Temple, and Paul could sit in Tarsus.

But although it was true that the power to gather in the elect belonged to God, the tool that God would use turned out to be, not the angels in heaven, but the church on earth. And the early years of the church as recorded in The Acts is the story of God educating the people to that fact, pushing them even against their will into missionary activity, which they did not see as their own responsibility. The book of The Acts is the story of the Holy Spirit forcing the church into outreach. That is the significance of Peter going up to see Cornelius, the Roman officer. It is not by personal resolve but due to a vision of the Spirit and a command received in that vision that Peter goes to a Gentile (Acts 10:1 ff.). But despite this direct command of the Spirit to Peter, the church still does not see the implications, and instead, Peter, rather than precipitating the movement, is called before his peers and required to justify his actions (ch. 11:3 f.). The lesson is not learned, despite the fact that to another person, Philip, exactly the same lesson had been communicated. Earlier, divine envoys had commanded Philip to reach out (ch. 8:26), and the Holy Spirit himself had commanded him to speak to the Ethiopian (v. 29). Eventually it took a persecution to shake the church out of Jerusalem and turn it out into the world (vs. 1, 4), but even that did not include the apostles (v. 1).

Despite these interventions of the Spirit with Peter and Philip, the church was a reluctant learner and refused to heed the implications of these events. Thus it is that God settles on Paul as the instrument through whom he will work. First, Barnabas (who

Conversion and Voyages

is, significantly, called a *Spirit-filled* man, Acts 11:24) goes to Tarsus to seek Paul and bring him out of retirement. But then, while he is at Antioch, the climactic event takes place. In ch. 13:2, the Spirit speaks: "Set apart for me Barnabas and Saul for the work to which I have called them." The first missionary voyage begins, not by resolve of Paul, but by order of the Spirit.

Even when Paul begins that first voyage, he seems to have no full comprehension of what it means to be a missionary. This can be seen in two things. In the first place, he goes to Jews! Again and again, at every place he visits, he goes first to the synagogue and he turns to the Gentiles only when he has been rejected by the Jews. The implications of this fact are enormous. It becomes apparent that if the Jews had not rejected him, but had instead received him, he never would have turned to the Gentiles at all! This can be seen in that, even though he cries out, "Behold, we turn to the Gentiles" after being refused by Jews in one place (v. 46), at his very next port of call, he goes back once more to the synagogue (ch. 14:1)! His turning to the Gentiles is not an overall resolve for the conduct of his future work; it is simply a decision for that specific place (see ch. 13:5, at Salamis; v. 14, at Antioch; ch. 14:1, at Iconium; ch. 17:1, at Thessalonica; v. 17, at Athens; ch. 18:4, at Corinth; vs. 24 f., at Ephesus; and note also that the book of The Acts closes with Paul in earnest conversation *with Jews!*). If the Jews had received him, he would not have turned to Gentiles, so limited was his missionary vision. As a matter of fact, Paul flatly tells us that his turning to the Gentiles was simply a ruse, a means to an end, an attempt to arouse the Jews to jealousy and attract them into the church! (In Rom. 11:13 f., Paul says, "Inasmuch then as I am an apostle to the Gentiles, I magnify my ministry in order to make my fellow Jews jealous, and thus save some of them."[12])

[12] On these verses Nygren writes: "He knows that the best service that he can just now render to the Jews is to preach the gospel to the Gentiles;

It is clear that, at least at this stage of his ministry, Paul did not see his obligation to save all people of all lands.

Secondly, this fact can be further seen not only in the people to whom Paul turned, Jews, but in the lands to which he went and the length of time he stayed there. On his first journey, where does he go? Or, better, where ought he to go? Aflame with a missionary purpose, ought he to go to the teeming cities of Europe with their massed thousands, or ought he to go to the remote sparsely settled hinterlands of Asia Minor? We would assume that a driving compulsion would lead him to the big cities, and he would move from one to the other as rapidly as possible. But instead, he goes to Asia Minor, to tiny little towns that had no great significance in the ancient Roman world — places such as Lystra, Derbe, and Iconium. But then, to make it all the more striking, not only does he go there on his *first* journey but he *returns there on his second journey* and seems quite willing to stay there without moving on! (This lack of a sense of the necessity to move on stays with him — a full eighteen months at Corinth, a full three years at Ephesus; in both places, despite the fact that he felt the end was close, he settled down there and might even have stayed longer if eventual civil disturbances had not driven him out of town.) He returns, then, to these remote corners of Asia Minor, turning his back on the great capital cities of the empire in the west, and is quite content to roam the depopulated Anatolians, not once but twice. But it is at this period of his life that the Spirit acts again. It is the Holy Spirit that literally commands him (Acts 16:6) to stop confining himself to this remote corner of Asia Minor, and it is again the

---

for he thereby awakens the Jews to envy. . . . It is precisely with the Jews in mind that he regards his apostleship to the Gentiles so highly " (*op. cit.,* p. 396). Schweitzer writes substantially the same thing: " It is therefore to save Israel that Paul exercises his calling as an apostle to the Gentiles " (*Mysticism,* p. 184).

Conversion and Voyages

Spirit that bars passage to another equally remote corner, Bithynia (v. 7). Paul is literally forced to the west, toward Europe, by the Spirit, who will not allow him to cover the same territory over and over again. Finally, he is driven as far west as one can go in Asia Minor, the port city of Troas. Once more the Spirit intervenes, this time with the vision of the man from Macedonia imploring him to come over and help. Seeing this as the command of God and "concluding that God had called us to preach the gospel to them" (v. 10), Paul and his party set sail. Hence, finally, under the prodding of the Spirit, the church reaches into Europe and eventually to Rome, to the ends of the earth.

Paul, of course, is an intelligent man, and eventually he comprehends this pattern of events and its significance. He comes to see that the power of God will be used to gather in the elect, but that God will not use angels, but rather, men as his instruments. Later in his life the great Pauline phrases begin to appear — phrases such as Gal. 3:28, "There is neither Jew nor Greek, . . . for you are all one in Christ Jesus," and phrases such as Rom. 15:20, 24, where he wishes to preach in lands in which Christ has not already been proclaimed. But these epistles are written in his *third missionary journey,* when the prodding of the Spirit has at last opened his eyes. This is part of the religious genius of Paul — not that he was from the outset an overall strategist, but rather, that he was a man open to God's leading, willing to be used even when the paths in which God directed him were not the paths which he would have chosen by himself.

What conclusion can we draw from these facts about his theology? The same conclusion we drew in discussing his conversion, namely, that once more we see that the key actor is not Paul but the Holy Spirit. One cannot understand the theology of Paul unless one begins with the elemental fact that it is *theos logia* (a study of *God*). God is the actor, the center. The theology of Paul is an absolutely closed book unless the doctrine of the Holy

Spirit, God in action, is seen as the central hub from which flows all of his thought. And again, to repeat the obvious, this is the Satanward view — the insistence that man is open to the interference of supernatural forces external to him.

CHAPTER 4

Paul's View of Sin and Man

SIN CAN BE DEFINED in one of three ways. And each of these three views has implications for a person's understanding of the nature of man, the work of Christ, and the nature of God.

First, sin can be defined as rebellion. This is the oldest Biblical understanding of the nature of sin. Adam is in the garden, rebelling, refusing to take orders, eating the forbidden fruit, rejecting the command of God. One sees, immediately, that in so defining sin, one has defined man. Man is free, responsible, and self-determining; man abuses his freedom and sets himself up as an enemy of God. The answer to sin is also predetermined. If sin is rebellion, the answer to rebellion is, obviously, to set aside that rebellion, to be sorry for one's rebellion, and to resolve to do it no more. Or, to use the theological term, one must repent and be reconciled. Repentance and reconciliation are the answers to rebellion. One could extend this by asking, What is it that makes man repent and be reconciled? What aspect of God's nature would here be stressed? God's power, forcing man to repent? Or God's love, wooing man back, making him wish of his own free will to turn from rebellion? Obviously the answer is God's love. To stress his power, obligating man to turn back, is to negate the whole proposition of man as free and responsible for his actions. When one speaks of sin as rebellion, that which will be immediately to the fore is a corresponding stress on God's love.[1]

Second, sin can be defined as guilt. Rebellion and guilt are closely associated, but they are not synonymous. They have a cause-effect relationship but nonetheless, they are separate entities in Biblical thought. There is a WET PAINT sign (to use a weak example) advising DO NOT TOUCH. I touch; that is my rebellion. My fingers are stained; that is my guilt. Rebellion is the act. Guilt is the consequence of the act. The stain remains even when the act is finished or rejected. All law recognizes the difference. If a man is a murderer (to use another weak example) and comes before the judge and says, "I am truly sorry; I will never do it again," the judge, even if he were able to be fully certain that the repentance was sincere and the resolve not to repeat the act certain, would not excuse the murder. He would not, for the man is not only a rebel against the laws of society, he is a guilty rebel. Saying, "I am sorry," and being repentant is not enough. Not only must his rebellion be dealt with, but all of the consequent guilt. And that guilt is dealt with either by execution or by long years of incarceration in prison. It is an axiom of law that guilt must be dealt with, a price must be paid, or it must be covered over, forgiven.

Because of the close relationship of rebellion and guilt, it is obvious that they both presuppose the same image of man as responsible, held to account for his past actions. What, then, is the answer to sin and guilt? The stained fingers must be cleansed, the guilt paid for and covered over. And the theological word for

---

[1] This can be seen in a passage such as Rom. 5:8 ff. Here Paul speaks of men as "enemies" of God, and he speaks of God's love and of reconciliation. That all three of these motifs should be clustered together in one brief span of a few verses indicates the way in which these motifs interlock. This is especially evident when one realizes that these motifs — man's enmity, God's love, and reconciliation — are not terms widely used in Paul, as we shall see in the course of this chapter.

Paul's View of Sin and Man

covering over, being washed in the blood of the lamb, is "atonement." Another way of saying this is to speak of forgiveness. Forgiveness does not mean that God condones or ignores the act, but it means that he atones or he himself pays the price of that guilt. Forgiveness, then, is not God's shutting his eyes to men's wrong, but rather, God's bearing our guilt in our place, and thus forgiving man's guilt, "he himself bore our sins in his body on the tree" (I Peter 2:24). From this point of view, notice once more that we are stressing God's love. He goes to the execution block in our place because "he cares about you" (ch. 5:7).

Third, sin can be defined not only as an act and a consequence of an act of a responsible man. It can be defined also in entirely different terms as a condition of man — a condition of slavery forced upon us by evil celestial forces outside of us, forces too great for us to resist. Sin can be defined as bondage under Satan. Sin can be personified, written with a capital *S,* the Sin, a tyrant who enters into us and holds us helpless against our will. Here is the picture out of the Synoptic Gospels of the demoniacs, people under the power of evil, rolling in the fire, beating themselves with chains, being consumed by overwhelming forces. Jesus has compassion upon them, recognizing that they are overwhelmed by superior evil forces they could not resist. He does not see them as supremely evil people who had sold their souls to evil and thus merit their fate, but he sees them as supremely unfortunate people, victims, against their will, of tyrannical forces.

One has, in this view, already made a statement about man. Man is helpless, a slave, in bondage to evil powers, or, as Luther put it in his liturgy, "We poor sinners confess unto thee that we are *by nature* sinful and unclean." And the answer to sin so conceived is not repentance. Saying, "I am sorry" accomplishes nothing. Nor is the answer forgiveness, for we are this way by nature and there is nothing for which we are personally guilty, needing forgiveness. The answer is, instead, salvation, freedom, rescue, being wrenched free from this evil power. This is the view from which the great gospel word *sōzō* comes, rescue from Satan, restoration unto wholeness.

From this point of view the emphasis upon the nature of God would stress, not his love, but his power. It is the superiority of God that counts. He is stronger than Satan and able to set man free. It is not that God's love is unimportant. If he were not love, he would not attempt our rescue. But, nonetheless, the stress is on his power, not his love. For if he were not superior, able to effectuate that love in rescue, then that love becomes meaningless, and we remain in bondage.

It must be recognized that repentance and reconciliation, forgiveness and atonement, and salvation or rescue are not synonyms. The words are not to be equated or used interchangeably as is often carelessly done. Each of them is part of a clearly defined circle of ideas extending to one's concept of sin, of man, and of God. These observations may be put into tabular form.

	Sin	Man	Answer to Sin	Nature of God
GODWARD	Rebellion	Free Responsible Enemy of God	Repentance Reconciliation	Love
	Guilt	Free Guilty Unclean	Forgiveness Atonement	Love
SATANWARD	Bondage A Tyrant	A slave	Salvation Freedom Rescue	Power

With the chart in front of us, we can examine this terminology, seeking to see (1) if Paul does speak in all three categories and

Paul's View of Sin and Man

(2), if he does, which of the three receives primary attention.

Because the terminology related to sin as guilt is the most weakly represented in Pauline vocabulary, we begin there and move on to the others in ascending order of frequency. Paul does use the Greek verbs meaning "to forgive." But that is not the primary thrust of his thinking. This is seen in the fact that although he does use these words, he uses them only rarely. For example, the primary verb for forgiveness (*aphiēmi*) is used only five times in all his epistles. This number is reduced by the fact that in one instance (Rom. 1:28) it means, not "to forgive," but rather, "to abandon or give up." Three more of the uses (I Cor. 7:11, 12, 13) have a similar idea of abandonment, and the Revised Standard Version rightly translates "to divorce." In only one instance does Paul use the verb in the sense of "to forgive" (Rom. 4:7). But even here it must be recognized that Paul is not speaking on his own but is quoting an Old Testament passage! In short, the only time Paul uses the verb "to forgive" is when he is constrained to do so by Old Testament material he is using. The noun *aphesis* receives the same sparing treatment. Only twice is it used (Eph. 1:7 and Col. 1:14), and even here it is obvious that the two verses are copies one of the other; so, in effect, we have not two uses, but one repeated. Nor is the circle greatly increased when we turn to another word that could be translated "to forgive," *charizomai*. Paul uses the word fifteen times, and of those fifteen, a full six must be translated, not "to forgive," but rather, "to bestow, grant, or give" (Rom. 8:32; I Cor. 2:12; Gal. 3:18; Phil. 1:29; 2:9; and Philemon 22). Thus in only nine instances can the verb rightly be translated "to forgive," and of those nine one is pure irony or sarcasm (II Cor. 12:13), and five others refer, not to God's forgiveness, but to the forgiveness that Christians extend one to the other (II Cor. 2:7, 10; Eph. 4:32; and Col. 3:13). And even in two of these three remaining uses (Eph. 4:32 and Col. 3:13), there is serious doubt as to whether the term is really to be translated to forgive, or might better be translated in the sense of being gracious.[2] In short, there is a paucity of language of forgiveness, and here Paul shows himself true to the pattern established by Jesus.[3] In effect, we can see that although the motif of forgiveness is real in Paul, it is not a dominant stream of his thought.

The same truth can be seen by examining the accompanying concept of man — man as guilty or unclean. The thought is present in Paul — but barely. Only once, in Rom. 3:19, does he call man *hypodikos* (to be liable to judgment or guilty). And only once does he use the like term *enochos* (I Cor. 11:27), which also

[2] Vincent Taylor comments on these two verses: "Moffatt renders the former 'be generous to each other' and the same meaning suits both passages. . . . It is in harmony with this claim that nowhere else does Paul summarize the blessings which Christ confers upon men under the idea of forgiveness" (*Forgiveness and Reconciliation*, p. 7).

[3] Again we quote Taylor, for in an incisive paragraph he has clearly stated the oft-overlooked fact that forgiveness is not central either in Paul *or in the Synoptics:* "If we omit parallels in the various gospels and in the different sources we are left with five sayings: those on blasphemy, on forgiving others, and on repeated forgiveness, that in the Lord's Prayer, and the word from the cross; and in addition the reference to forgiveness in the Lukan story of the woman (7:47) and in the Matthew parable of the unforgiving servant. The material is less, I think than might have been expected. . . . The absence of a saying of Jesus directly associating His death with forgiveness is a confirmation that . . . the forgiveness of sins is not the primary object of His suffering and death" (*Forgiveness and Reconciliation*, pp. 13-14). Paul, Taylor recognizes, follows in the same stream: "Concerning forgiveness he [Paul] has very little to say and he never represents it as the object for which Christ died" (*Atonement*, p. 120). There simply is no sacrificial interpretation of the death of Jesus worked out in detail in either the Synoptics or Paul. Sacrificial imagery and allusions abound. But there is no attempt made to organize them in Levitical terms as a satisfaction made unto God. Davies, in his work on Paul, sees this: "We are compelled to recognize not only from the paucity of his use of such terms and concepts but also from his obvious inability to enter into the full spiritual significance of the sacrificial system . . . that although his thought can move along the channels of sacrifice, yet the latter are not fully native to him, as it were" (*op. cit.*, p. 250).

Paul's View of Sin and Man

means liable to judgment or guilty. Nor does the circle widen when one turns to terms of man as unclean or impure. For example, Paul uses the word *akathartos* (unclean or impure) only twice (I Cor. 7:14; II Cor. 6:17). But even here, one can see clearly, especially in the I Cor. 7:14 reference, that Paul has moved away from the sacrificial language of payment for guilt and has instead entered into Satanward terminology. This can be seen in two ways. First, there is the Synoptic background of *akathartos*. It is used nineteen times in the Synoptics and in every instance, without exception, the adjective is used to qualify a demon, a member of the Satanic host. Second, the very way in which Paul develops his thought in I Cor., ch. 7, makes it clear that he is not speaking in juridical or sacrificial terms.[4] It is not our intent to deny that Paul sees man as unclean, but rather, to insist that although he does speak of man in this way, it is only sparingly. This can further be seen in that although he uses words such as *anomia* and *adikia*, he uses them only rarely. Hence, one can say that this stream of thought of sin as guilt is part of Paul's vocabulary, but not a central or formative part.

The same thing can be said of Paul's language in respect to sin as rebellion. Terms such as repentance, reconciliation, enmity, man as responsible, etc., are used with a greater frequency than the terms related to sin as guilt, but even though more widespread, statistics alone reveal that this is not the central stream of Pauline thought.[5] For example, *metanoeō*, which is the ob-

---

[4] See below, pp. 96–97.

[5] This fact, that terms of reconciliation are used with greater frequency than terms of forgiveness, leads Taylor to conclude that "the best New Testament word to describe the purpose of the atonement is Reconciliation. It is true that this word is used only in Paul" (*Atonement*, p. 279). (The thought is not original with Taylor. In *The Theology of the Epistles* [Gerald Duckworth & Co., Ltd., London, 1934], p. 134. H. A. A. Kennedy wrote: "J. Weiss may be right in asserting that the most comprehensive description of salvation in Paul is reconciliation.") Taylor's Biblical scholarship has already shown him that it is impossible to put the motif of for-

verse side of rebellion, is used only once in all of Paul (II Cor. 12:21). The noun does not fare much better. It is used only three times (Rom. 2:4; II Cor. 7:9 and 10). (It is also in this II Cor., ch. 7, context that we have Paul's only employment of *metamelomai,* and this is used in a nonreligious sense of being sorry.)

The family of words *apokatallassō, katallassō,* and *katallagē* fare somewhat better — but not much. The first word is used in Eph. 2:16 and twice in Col. 1:20-22. But in Colossians those who are reconciled are, at least in part, not men, but cosmic figures "in heaven."[6] The noun and verb *katallassō* and *katallagē* are found, in all of Paul, in only two places (Rom. 5:10-11 and II Cor. 5:18-20). Neither noun nor verb is ever used again by Paul outside these two contexts, except in I Cor. 7:11 in a strictly secular sense.

The idea of man as an enemy of God, a responsible enemy, is found in Paul, but is not a dominant theme. The word *echthros* is used nine times in Paul, but of these nine there are three that fall out of consideration — Rom. 12:20 and II Thess. 3:15, which refer to human enemies and not man's hostility to God, and Gal. 4:16, where Paul poses the rhetorical question, Am I your enemy? Of the remaining six uses, at least two refer, not to man as the enemy, but to cosmic figures who are enemies of God (I Cor. 15:25, 26). The word *echthra* is equally limited, used only four times by Paul. Further, the idea of man as responsible is affirmed in the *anapologētos* of Rom. 2:1, man is "without excuse." But

---

giveness at the center of Paul's thought (note 3 of this chapter); he has already rejected the motif of sin as slavery with its emphasis upon redemption or salvation (Ch. 2, n. 4, above); hence, all that is left to him is this stress on reconciliation despite his own observation that this "best New Testament word" is used only in Paul. This fact, that the word is used only in Paul, ought to be even more disconcerting to Taylor in the light of the fact that even in Paul the term is rarely used and in no sense can be considered formative (see the statistics that follow in this chapter).

[6] A fact that is not without its own significance. See below, Ch. 7, n. 15.

Paul's View of Sin and Man

this too is a very limited term, used by Paul only one other time (Rom. 1:20).

In short, one can say the same thing about this motif of sin as rebellion and its companion terms as we said in respect to sin as guilt with its companion terms. This is a real aspect of Paul's thought, but the paucity of terms will not allow us to conclude that it is the determinative aspect of Paul's theology. It is strictly a secondary stream of his consciousness.

It is not until we move into the last category, that Satanward motif, that the floodgates boom open, and we find ourselves in the full current of Pauline vocabulary. All of a sudden, where this or that word was used sparingly before, we find ourselves in a veritable torrent of words verifying the centrality of this motif. For example, the noun *doulos* is used twenty-three times. The verb *douleuō* (to serve as a slave) is used fifteen more times, and the similar verb *douloō* another five times. The compound verb *katadouloō* is used twice. Thus, the idea of man as enslaved is thrust upon us. Whereas the terms of reconciliation and forgiveness were sparse, the terms of liberation, of rescue and freedom, abound. The word *sōzō* alone is used twenty-one times, the noun *sōtēria* another seventeen times, and the title *sōtēr* is used again twice more. The verb *hruomai* (to rescue from danger) is used seven times, and in I Thess. 1:10, Jesus is literally called *ho hruomenos* (the rescuing one). The term *apolutrōsis* (a ransoming or emancipation or liberation) is used seven times. The verb *agorazō* is used three times, and the even stronger verb *exagorazō*, an additional four times. The verb *eleutheroō* (to free) is used five times by Paul, and the corresponding noun *eleutheria,* six more times. One could continue, in Paul, almost indefinitely with the citing of further synonyms and statistics, but for one whose mind is open and working, it is already more than apparent that the enormous thrust of Paul's vocabulary is found within this Satanward stream of seeing sin as power, and the answer as being a saving intervention of an even more powerful God who sets man free.

In line with this, at least a glance must be given to the last column of our chart, the "Nature of God." It must be seen that for Paul the stress is unmistakably on God's power. It is true that Paul makes God the subject of *agapaō*, and the one to whom *agapē* toward men belongs. But it is not often that he uses these terms, nor does he use them in a formative way. In I Thess. 1:4 and II Thess. 2:13, he refers to the elect as the "beloved of God," but the participle is used in an undeveloped way as a simple title. It is only in Rom. 5:8 f. and in ch. 8:35 f., in all of Paul, that he develops the idea of God as love. It is only here that (1) God is seen as the subject of *agapaō*, or *agapē* is seen as belonging to God in respect to men, and (2) this love of God is linked to the death and resurrection of Jesus. Outside of these two contexts, every other employment of either verb or noun is in a context quite apart from the actual discussion of the redemptive work of Jesus. For example, there is the maxim of II Cor. 9:7, "God loves a cheerful giver," or the benediction of ch. 13:14, "the love of God," or the simple titles of Col. 3:12 and I Thess. 1:4, "beloved of God." It is, to repeat, only in the two Roman contexts that Paul relates the love of God to the redemptive work of Christ, and in the first context it is quite clear that this reference to the love of God is "although not incidental, . . . not the main thought."[7] In the second context, Rom. 8:35 f., it is quite clear that the love of God, though mentioned, is not mentioned in Godward terms of a love turning us away from our rebellion. Rather, the love of God is seen here in Satanward terms as a love that will not surrender us to the enemy. There is nothing in all of creation that can separate man from God. The powers and

---

[7] The quotation is from Taylor, *Atonement*, p. 104. Hence it is exceedingly significant, for as we have seen, Taylor is working within exclusively Godward categories of thought (see note 5 of this chapter).

Paul's View of Sin and Man

principalities can rain affliction upon the elect, but because of the superiority of God, they will not succeed in their diabolical attempt at establishing a division between God and his elect. There is a definite Satanward thrust to the passage. Thus Paul does not stress the love of God, and here too he stands squarely with Synoptic thought.[8]

It is no accident of expression that in precisely those places where Paul would emphasize the fullest meaning of God's action in Christ, he speaks not of God's love but of God's power — "the power of God for salvation" (Rom. 1:16); "the word of the cross . . . is the power of God" (I Cor. 1:18); "Christ the power of God" (v. 24). Again, lest we be misunderstood, it is not that the love of God is inconsequential or unimportant. Paul *does* make God the subject of the verb, but that love is significant simply because God is able to manifest his superiority. If the enemy of Rom. 8:35 were able to separate the elect from God, God's love would be meaningless. God's love is valuable because it is backed up by power — a power able to save man from sin as power, an invading tyrant.

This concept of sin as a tyrannical, enslaving force entering man even against man's will becomes even more sharply silhouetted when one makes a careful examination of the key word

[8] A fact, often overlooked, is that whereas men are often exhorted to love God in the Synoptics, there is not one single instance in the Synoptics where God is the subject of *agapaō*. In like manner, the noun *agapē* is used but twice in the Synoptics and never is it the *agapē of God*. The same thing is true of The Acts. Not only are *agapē* and *agapaō* not used of God, but they are not used *at all* in The Acts. The emphasis of the early sermons of The Acts is not on the love of God, but rather, on his power — his ability to overcome the strength of Satan seen in his wrenching Jesus back from the grave: "But God raised him up, having loosed the pangs of death" (Acts 2:24); "This Jesus God raised up, and of that we are all witnesses" (v. 32); "whom God raised from the dead. To this we are witnesses" (ch. 3:15); "And with great power the apostles gave their testimony to the resurrection of the Lord Jesus" (ch. 4:33). This stress on the power of God seen in the resurrection is carried forward in Paul; see below, pp. 76-78.

for sin, *hamartia*. Paul uses this word (if we accept the variant reading of I Thess. 2:3) fifty-nine times. Of these fifty-nine times, only ten can definitely be considered as indicating sin as rebellion or guilt. In I Cor. 15:3, we have the term in the plural, and it quite obviously means rebellious acts or their consequent guilt. The same thought is found in I Cor. 15:17; Gal. 1:4; Eph. 2:1; Col. 1:14; and I Thess. 2:16. In II Cor. 11:7, the term is used in the singular, but again it obviously refers to an individual act of the human personality. However, in all of Romans (and it is in that epistle that the word *hamartia* is primarily found — a full forty-five of Paul's fifty-nine usages being confined to this epistle alone), there are only three places where the word can rightly be seen as referring to either human guilt or human rebellion, and each of these three places is not an ordinary expression of Paul, but rather, a place where he is quoting from the Old Testament and is thus limited by the language he is reproducing (Rom. 4:7, 8; 11:27). In every other instance, the word " sin " should rightfully be translated The Sin, for it is seen as an objective force, a personification, a tyrant, an enslaving master that enters man and rules against man's will. In Rom. 5:12, The Sin enters the world as an invading force, patrolling. In v. 21, it is actually spoken of as reigning. In ch. 6:6 men are enslaved by Sin. In vs. 16, 17, and 20, The Sin and slavery are linked together. The obverse side of this — men being freed from or released from this tyrant — is spoken of in vs. 7, 11, 18, 22, etc. In v. 23, the tyrant Sin is seen as paying a wage, Death. This idea of Sin reigning in Death is seen also in I Cor. 15:56 and Rom. 5:21.[9] In Rom. 7:8 and 11, the parallel between Sin and the depiction of Satan is quite remarkable. Whereas in I Cor. 7:5, Satan is seen as hovering, waiting for an opening through which to attack, in the two verses in Romans, Sin is seen as seeking an occasion, working

[9] This interdependence of Sin and Death is remarked upon by Dibelius in a telling phrase. He speaks of them as Mr. and Mrs., " they go together."

Paul's View of Sin and Man

through the law, waiting for an opportunity to attack. In Rom. 7:14, Paul speaks of being sold under Sin, helpless under its power, and the same idea of Sin as an enslaving tyrant invading him and overpowering him against his will is clearly and explicitly stated in both vs. 17 and 20, where Paul flatly differentiates between himself and The Sin, sandwiching the two references around the statement of his own helplessness: "I can will what is right, but I cannot do it" (v. 18). The obvious intent of Paul's language — to recognize sin, not as an act of man, but as an enslaving power — has been fully recognized by contemporary theology.[10] What is lacking is not the motif's recognition, but

---

[10] Nygren writes: "To Paul sin is not basically separate moral missteps; but *sin is a power under whose bondage man lives*" (*op. cit.*, p. 242). Walter Grundmann, writing in Gerhard Kittel, *Bible Key Words,* "Sin" (Harper & Row, Publishers, Inc., 1951), p. 80, comments on Rom., ch. 7, "Man's inner conflict is to be understood in terms of demonic possession." H. A. A. Kennedy writes: "It is important to notice that Paul usually speaks of sin not as an individual transgression nor as abstract tendency to wrong doing, but as a quasi-personal power which takes possession of human nature and leads it astray" (*op. cit.,* p. 33). In *Paul* (The Westminster Press, 1953), p. 111, Martin Dibelius writes: "Within the framework of his theological thought, Paul speaks of sin in the singular, and sometimes it sounds as if it were a living being, a tyrant dominating the human race (Rom. 5:12-21), or a demon manifesting itself in the human heart (Rom. 7:7-25). . . . He is, in a way, infected, so that even his piety, his striving after righteousness, and his knowledge of what is good turn to evil in him." Barrett insists that the meaning of Rom. 6:14 is: "Sin shall not dominate over you . . . might almost be translated, sin shall not be your lord," and he further adds: "Paul assumes that men will be slaves and obedient, to a good master or a bad. Independence is impossible" (*op. cit.,* pp. 128-132). Wrede writes: "Paul regards men as held in bondage under objective powers of evil; namely, first of all, the flesh, sin, the law, death. These are no mere abstract or metaphorical expressions but Wesenheiten, realities, active forces" (quoted by Gustav Aulén, *Christus Victor,* p. 65; The Macmillan Company, 1951). Klausner writes: "Sin is, for Paul, like death, an inexhaustible heritage of the human race. Sin enfolds us all without exception, from the womb to the grave. . . . Sin comes from the persuasions and enticements of those 'powers of darkness,' those evil spirits with Satan as their head. . . . Sin rules in man and

its acceptance and application.[11]

We have gone far enough in these statistical studies to have seen that for Paul, that which is fundamental and determinative is the idea of sin as slavery, the Satanward view. We can now go on to ask ourselves, How does Paul understand Christ to have dealt with sin in its three forms?

How does Jesus overcome guilt? The answer is simply given in I Cor. 15:3, "Christ died for our sins." Here Paul is insisting that Jesus overcomes guilt by taking our place at the judgment bar of God. Guilt demands a price; it cannot be ignored in the holiness of God. Guilt must not be condoned, but atoned. "For our sake he [God] made him [Jesus] to be sin who knew no sin, so that in him we might become the righteousness of God." (II

---

has dominion over him and man does not have the power to oppose those evil powers of darkness" (*op. cit.*, p. 521). C. A. Anderson Scott writes: "Paul's treatment of the subject of sin is largely governed by his conception of it as something objective and external. . . . To this personified external force man has come to be in servitude. . . . It is not enough to say as is commonly done, that in these and other passages, Paul comes near to *personifying* sin. He came near to personifying it because he conceived it as something which had existence and showed activity prior to and independent of his consent to it. And conversely we do not find any indication of sin (in the singular) being conceived of as individual and personal. Paul does not speak, as we should do, of 'my sin,' meaning sinful condition. . . . 'Sin' is not for him a synonym for a sinful status; it is a pp. 46–47). The affirmation of this motif could be continued through several more pages of quotations.

[11] For example, Grundmann, quoted in note 10 of this chapter, where he sees sin as an invading power, can immediately pass on to negate his own insight, insisting: "All his [Paul's] references to demons and to Satan are meant to give actuality to his teaching about sin; they are not the outcome of dualistic speculation. . . . The true nature of sin is thus made clear; it is man's self-assertion in rebellion against God" (*loc. cit.*, pp. 78–80). Kennedy, remarking that Sin is a personal power forcing man astray, can nonetheless conclude: "Sin is essentially self-will" (*op. cit.*, p. 35). Similar attempts to repudiate the evidence of their own findings are found in most theologians.

Paul's View of Sin and Man

Cor. 5:21.) The idea of substitution is here. God pours out his wrath, not on us, but on Jesus. Jesus bears the punishment in our place. This is the meaning of Rom. 3:25, where Jesus is called an expiation or a covering over for the guilt of men.[12] This is about all that Paul has to say on this motif. Because of the failure of Paul to develop this motif further, he has been accused by some of not being a theologian.[13] But the simple fact is that that is all that has to be said. Paul does not dwell on this motif further because it is not primary to his thought. Sin as guilt is strictly a secondary stream of his consciousness.

How does Jesus overcome sin as rebellion? This too is dealt with in a very cursory fashion by Paul because it is also a secondary stream of his thought. But even though cursory, Paul's remarks are incisive and complete. Jesus overcomes rebellion in two ways. First, he overcomes rebellion by not being rebellious himself. He, a true man, lives a life free of rebellion. To understand this, it must be seen how the pieces of the Godward view fit together. The stress here is on the humanity of Jesus, in speaking of his overcoming of both guilt and rebellion. He is identified with sinful humanity, a true man, subordinate to the Father. In Phil. 2:7, Jesus is defined as "being born in the likeness of men," and the term is *homoiōmati*, used also in Rom. 8:3. The term is poorly translated as "likeness," for that accentuates the idea of difference as much as it does solidarity. But Paul is stress-

---

[12] We accept Schweitzer's remark on this passage as valid: "Attempts to deny the existence in this passage of the conception of a satisfaction offered by Christ to God, such as have been made by Albrecht Ritschl and others are impossible to carry through" (*Mysticism*, p. 217).

[13] Taylor is one who adopts this view of Paul: "A profound thinker, he is not a constructive theologian anxious to build up a comprehensive theory of the meaning of the death of Christ" (*Atonement*, p. 95). What Taylor means, of course, is that he does not understand Paul and can make no sense out of him precisely because he is searching in minor streams of thought for that which is fundamental, seeing in "reconciliation" the heart of Pauline teaching. (See note 3 of this chapter.)

ing not Jesus' similarity to the race, but his absolute oneness with it.[14] There is a sharp stress on the subordination of Jesus to the Father, and this same stress can be seen elsewhere also (I Cor. 15:28). Having emphasized the true humanity of Jesus, we are led on to see how the true human Jesus overcomes sin as rebellion, first, as we have said, by himself not rebelling. That is the thought of the Phil. 2:5 passage, where Jesus is defined as being one with the race. He "became obedient unto death, even death on a cross" (v. 8). Thus Jesus overcomes sin as rebellion by living a life, as man, free of all rebellion. But secondly, Jesus also overcomes rebellion by his example. By showing us a pattern, he gives us a model to follow. Just as he was obedient, so also, the passage begins, are we to be the same: "Have this mind among yourselves, which you have in Christ Jesus" (v. 5). This, then, is how Paul sees Jesus as overcoming rebellion. One, by leading a life free of rebellion himself, and two, by serving as example and model for those who follow him, who are to do likewise. Again, it is not a widely developed concept, for Paul's main thrust lies elsewhere, and the *imitatio Christi* motif is never a highly developed thought in Paul.[15]

[14] Barrett writes: "The word 'form' or 'likeness' has already been used several times . . . and in none of these places does it mean simply 'imitation.' . . . We are probably justified therefore in our translation, and in deducing that Christ took precisely that same fallen nature that we ourselves have" (*op. cit.,* p. 156).

[15] When Davies writes that "the imitation of Christ is part and parcel of Paul's ethic" (*op. cit.,* p. 147), Davies is wrong. Nock is much closer to the truth when he comments: "Paul only thrice commends the imitation of Christ, I Thess. 1:6, Rom. 15:7, Col. 3:13. . . . Normal Christian life, however, was not a matter of imitating Jesus, but was life by the Spirit of Christ" (*op. cit.,* p. 244). This fact that the Christian life is not produced by individual resolve to live like Jesus, but is instead a product of the Spirit active within us, will be dealt with in detail later (see below, pp. 103–105), and this fact that the good life is not man's doing, but God's accomplishment in man is what accounts for the otherwise true but inexplicable observation of Bultmann: "There are no special practices desig-

Paul's View of Sin and Man

The primary stress of Paul's thought as to the work of Jesus in overcoming sin rests with his overcoming of sin as slavery — the Satanward view. And I shall develop this in later chapters. For the moment, however, something else of profound importance must be noted: the Satanward view is wider in scope than the work of overcoming sin. Sin is only one of many tyrants that rule over man's life, racking him with adversity. Contemporary theology is stultified. It concentrates upon sin to an extent and a degree that is non-Pauline. Sin, for Paul, was not a central idea. And here too Paul stands squarely in the Synoptic tradition.[16]

Although it is true that contemporary Christian theology explains the work of Christ almost exclusively in terms of setting man free from sin (no matter how the term may be understood), it is highly disquieting to recognize the fact, which cannot be ignored by one who reads through the Pauline epistles, that Paul himself does not place sin at the center of his thought in respect to the work of Christ. If one used military language (something that Paul does often), one could say that sin is seen, not as the only enemy, nor even as the major enemy, but instead, as only one minor member of a gigantic cosmic host of evil powers that holds man enslaved.

This can be seen by running very quickly through the Pauline epistles. In I and II Thessalonians together, *hamartia* appears only twice, and *hamartanō* and *hamartōlos* not at all. In these earliest epistles the major problem for the Thessalonians is not sin but *suffering*, and the fact that *death* continued. The fact that sin continued in their lives seems to be no problem for them.

---

nated for the man of faith, Gal. 5:6; . . . and that means also, no specifically religious practices" (*op. cit.*, p. 324). Paul gives no ethical instruction or program of *imitatio Christi*, because right ethical activity was not an accomplishment of man, but a work of the Spirit.

[16] Again, this is a thought often noticed but never developed. Grundmann remarks: "It is remarkable how small a part is played by ideas about sin in the synoptic gospels" (*loc. cit.*, p. 64).

What does concern them is that some of their number are dying and all are suffering. Further, it is in these epistles that the major enemy described by Paul is the *lawless one,* the great cosmic figure upheld by the power of Satan (II Thess. 2:9), and thus Paul reassures them that at the Second Coming of Christ Jesus this enemy will be slain by the breath of his mouth (v. 8). Suffering, death, Satan, the lawless one, are the enemies from which the church yearns for release.

And the same thing is true in Galatians. In the whole epistle Paul barely even mentions the fact of sin, using *hamartia* only three times. This is an astounding fact. Paul spends a whole epistle speaking of the redemptive work of Christ, liberating men, and crying out in Gal. 5:1, even at the risk of being redundant, that "for freedom Christ has set us free," and yet sin is absolutely peripheral to his thought at this point. The real enemy from from which Christ has freed men is *the law* (ch. 3:13).[17] Furthermore, in Galatians the enemy is not only the law but even more, the evil celestial forces who stand behind the law, *the weak and beggarly elemental spirits of the universe* (ch. 4:8-9). It is into their bondage that the Galatians are returning anew by embracing the law.

The same is true of the Corinthian literature. Sin just is not the major target of Christ's work. In I Cor. 2:8, Paul explicitly says that the death of Jesus was due to the *rulers of this age,* headed by Satan, who is the "god of this world" (II Cor. 4:4). Furthermore, Paul flatly insists that the major or last or greatest enemy is not sin, but *death* (I Cor. 15:26). It is because death is the greatest of all enemies that the resurrection is the vital center of his thought (vs. 14, 17). The resurrection is important because it is historical proof that the greatest of the enemy arsenal, death, is no match for Christ's power.[18]

[17] See Schweitzer's quotation, Ch. 3, n. 2, above.
[18] See below, pp. 77–78.

Paul's View of Sin and Man

Only in Romans is *sin* seen as a formative term (we have already noted that forty-five of Paul's fifty-nine usages of this term are in this epistle alone — outside of Romans the term is rare). Once one has moved out of Romans into the later epistles, sin is left behind as a basic factor, and once more the cosmic foes return, as in Eph. 6:12. Having made reference to the *devil* in the preceding sentence, Paul goes on to say, " For we are not contending against flesh and blood, but against the *principalities,* against the *powers,* against the *world rulers* of this present darkness, against the *spiritual hosts of wickedness* in the heavenly places." To repeat, it is only in Romans that sin is a fundamental term, but even the word in Romans must be carefully measured against the fact that in that epistle too these same *principalities* and *powers* and *death* are seeking to sunder the elect from God (Rom. 8:35 f.). And further, as we have already seen, it is in Romans that the primary thrust of Paul's employment of the term " sin " represents, not human rebellion and consequent guilt, but an enslaving force external to man who invades man against man's will.

Something disturbing has happened in contemporary New Testament theology. If all the enemies Paul mentions were ranged in order, their listing would appear like this:

1. Suffering
2. Death
3. The lawless one
4. Satan
5. The law
6. The weak and beggarly elemental spirits
7. The rulers of this age
8. The god of this world
9. Sin
    a. Primary meaning: tyrant
    b. Secondary meaning: rebellion and guilt

10. The devil
11. Principalities and powers
12. World rulers
13. Spiritual hosts of wickedness

What has happened is that Pauline theology today is truncated and abridged, and consequently grossly misleading. It is truncated and abridged because out of the whole host of enemies Paul's thought sees as ranged against us, theology has settled on only one minor member, sin, and in developing that minor member's meaning, it has settled on the secondary and nonformative way in which the term is used. All we speak of today is Christ overcoming rebellion and paying the price of guilt. This is misleading because the end result has been to subjectivize the Christian message, reducing it to a psychological internal experience of the individual, rather than seeing that message as an objective proclamation of the superiority of God over all forces that stand ranged against man. Evil is not to be reduced to existential bad intentions. And theology has done that, and has thus rendered itself irrelevant.[19]

[19] This line of thought will be continued in the final chapter.

CHAPTER 5

Paul's View of the Church, the New Creation, and Salvation

IN THE FIRST CHAPTER, I insisted that Paul means exactly the same thing by the term "salvation" that Jesus does by the phrase "the Kingdom of God." Then, in Chapter 4, we began looking at the work of Jesus, seeing how it produced repentance and reconciliation, and atonement and forgiveness. But we also noted that although those are real motifs, Paul's primary emphasis rests with the words "salvation," "freedom," "redemption," etc. We continue that discussion in this chapter.

The place to begin is by reminding ourselves of verses we have already glanced at in passing. Paul insists that this world is under the control of celestial tyrants.[1] These tyrants include those listed at the close of the last chapter (elemental spirits, sin, death, the devil, etc.), and as evidence of Paul's view, one can cite I Cor. 2:8 ("the rulers of this age"); Eph. 6:12 ("the world rulers"); II Cor. 4:4 ("the god of this world"), etc. It is because this age is under evil powers that it is the "present *evil* age" (Gal. 1:4).

---

[1] Bultmann, in his own incisive style, affirms this: "When Rom. 8:20 speaks of the 'creation' subject to transitoriness and longing for freedom . . . it presupposes that there is an area of the creation in which rebellious powers, at enmity with God and man, hold sway. Thus the creation has a peculiarly ambiguous character: on the one hand, it is the earth placed by God at man's disposal for his use and benefit . . . on the other, it is the field of activity of evil demonic powers" (*op. cit.*, p. 230).

The cosmos itself is enslaved to these evil powers, or, as Paul says in Rom. 8:21, the world process itself, the physical cosmos, is in bondage to decay.

Now, since this cosmos itself is in bondage, depressed under evil forces, the essential content of the word "salvation" is that the world itself will be rescued, or renewed, or set free. Salvation is a cosmic event affecting the whole creation. It is not simply the internal renewal of man's religious attitude. It is not a psychological openness to the future, or a heightened consciousness of God's presence. It is instead a rescue of the whole world. Salvation is not simply the overcoming of my rebellion and the forgiveness of my guilt, but salvation is the liberation of the whole world process, of which I am only a small part.[2] This is precisely what Paul is insisting in the Rom., ch. 8, passage: "The creation waits with eager longing" for the revelation of the sons of God. But the creation waits not merely as spectator but also as par-

[2] The loss of this insight has meant that redemption has come to be seen as a personal affair, an individual thing. Man has thrust himself to the center of the stage. Since Luther's great dictum, "How can I find peace with God?" the basic thrust of redemption has been understood in personal, egocentric terms. Despite the fact that Luther's approach to Romans is theocentric, his approach to salvation is egocentric. Whether salvation is attributed to God alone, as Luther saw it, is beside the point. The real issue is that man has managed to make himself and himself alone the focal point of the entire activity of God. He has insisted upon his own fundamental centrality. The whole spectrum of Protestant thought is egocentric. Whether one ranges from the one extreme of Calvinistic emphasis upon election to the other extreme of Pentecostal insistence upon man as responsible for a decision at a revival meeting, the basic truth remains the same in both camps, namely, that it is man, the individual, who is the prime focus of the work of God. Even in his theological structures man's sin is seen in that he insists he must be central. In the deepest sense, God is denied any independent existence — he exists only to serve and to save man, a celestial errand runner. This is why Protestant theology has never been able to come to any adequate theology of the church. But the Roman Catholic Church is in no happier a state. For Catholics too, salvation is an egocentric or personal affair, and the church is simply a means through which, in the many Sacraments, the grace of God can reach the individual.

The Church, the New Creation, Salvation

ticipant. The revelation of the sons of God will be also the time of its own cleansing, for the creation also was "subject to futility." Hence Paul writes, "The creation itself will be set free from its bondage to decay and obtain the glorious liberty of the children of God." It is a future event — a near future event in Paul's thought — and it is a physical event of the whole cosmos, not a spiritual event of the inner man. Using the imagery of a coming birth in the verses that immediately follow (Rom. 8:23 f.), he insists that the labor pains have already begun — that is how near he holds the event to be (and the shared nature of the event, the cosmos and the sons of God both participating, is seen in the prefix that Paul attaches to the verb for labor pains — man and the world groaning together).[3] But, even though it is very near, it is nonetheless, for Paul, still in the future,[4] and in this he stands shoulder to shoulder with Jesus.[5]

This, of course, at least to this point, is standard Jewish apoc-

[3] This concept of the world itself not being abandoned or ignored but instead being renewed is seen also in the I Cor. 7:29-31 context. There, it is not the *kosmos* but the *schēma tou kosmou* that is passing away. That is, it is not the world itself, but the "bearing, deportment, outward appearance" that is about to change. The world, in the immediate moment, is under evil *kosmokrateroi*, but that will change.

[4] We have already quoted C. A. Anderson Scott and C. K. Barrett to support our earlier claim that salvation is a formative word in Paul's vocabulary (see Ch. 1, n. 6, above). We quote them again to substantiate the claim not only that salvation is central to Paul but that it is a future event. Scott goes on to write: "Most commonly he [Paul] uses it in reference to the future with an eschatological significance" (*op. cit.*, p. 23). Barrett, in the very same paragraph as quoted earlier, goes on to say, "Salvation itself lies in the future," and then continues later (p. 107) to expand on the verb. "It belongs essentially to the future, and the verb 'to save' is here (Rom. 5:9), as usual in that future tense (so at 5:10, 9:27, 10:9, 13, 11:14, 11:26); at 11:14 it is possibly in the subjunctive (with future meaning); at 8:24 it is in the aorist indicative but qualified by 'in hope.'"

[5] For Jesus also, the present world as it stands shall pass away (Matt. 24:35) at the return of Jesus, the end of this age (v. 3).

alyptic thought. The present evil age, under the control of the devil, is to be succeeded by the future cleansed world, under the control of God.

Jesus enters this fallen world. He becomes "identical" with man.[6] That is, he enters into this planet which is languishing under the control of the god of this world, Satan. That makes Jesus a slave of Satan, a subject of his realm. Not a servant, executing Satan's will, but a slave exposed to his evil will. That is precisely what Paul calls Jesus in his incarnate life, a slave, *doulos* (Phil. 2:7). This verse is ordinarily translated by theologians as indicating that in the incarnation, Jesus became a servant of God, but although that is a truly Pauline idea, that does not exhaust the meaning here. It is not the basic thought at this point. For one thing, it just does not say a servant of God — the "of God" part does not even fit the context. Jesus is in the likeness of men — that is the primary thrust — and men are not characterized anywhere in Paul's thought as servants of God, but rather, as slaves of Satan, helpless and in bondage. And Jesus is identified with men in that bondage. He is not a servant of God but a slave of Satan.[7] The whole context makes this clear, and this is precisely what gives meaning to the two antithetical halves of the passage. He is at first a slave under Satan and the evil powers, and their will is worked on him; but then the roles are reversed and he is above the evil powers. At a later time they are obliged to bow before him. It is this reversal of roles which Paul develops in Phil. 2:10 f., where he insists that every knee, on earth and above the earth, and under the earth, shall bow before him, and every tongue shall be obliged to confess him as

---

[6] See above, pp. 67–68, and Ch. 4, n. 14.

[7] J. A. T. Robinson is one of the few who flatly affirm this meaning of Phil. 2:7. In *The Body* (London: SCM Press, Ltd., 1957), p. 38, he writes: "The reference here is not merely to Jesus' lowly status on earth. It means that by assuming sarx, He accepted the position of being a 'doulos' (strictly a 'slave born') to the 'powers,' in the likeness of all men who are 'enslaved under the elemental spirits of the world' (Gal. 4:3)."

The Church, the New Creation, Salvation

Lord and acknowledge his supremacy. Jesus, the true man, in bondage to Satan, exposed to the attack of the world powers, goes on to triumph over them.

That Jesus goes on to triumph over them is the significance of the cross-resurrection event as Paul interprets it. Paul paints the cross as the place of combat. Notice how Paul insists, in Col. 2:14-15 (written at the same time of his life as Philippians), how the cross is the place where Jesus returns the attack of the evil forces. The idea of conflict is especially clear in v. 15. The Revised Standard Version translates the verse: "He disarmed the principalities and powers, and made a public example of them, triumphing over them in it" (marginal reading; not "in him," but "in it," the cross). We shall return to this verse in depth later on,[8] but for the moment we simply stress the obvious intent of the verse — that Paul is insisting upon this act as a place where Jesus exposes the impotency of the evil forces. He triumphs over them. Notice, from this point of view, the daring imagery of Paul in v. 14. The phrase " the bond . . . with its legal demands " is obscure. Apparently it refers to the law, the curse of the law to which Paul refers in Galatians (a parallel epistle).[9] But what is not at all obscure is this fact — that it is Jesus who does the nailing! It is he who stands, hammer in hand, nailing the legal demands of the law to the cross! This is what we mean when we say that Paul daringly reverses the whole imagery of the cross. It is Jesus who is attacking, triumphing over these evil powers. They attacked him. He was their slave, under their rule, exposed to their weapons, and they overestimated their capacities. He had gone about overcoming their weapons, in his miracles, beating back their bonds of sickness and suffering and hunger,[10] and they had decided to still him once and for all by hitting him with

---

[8] See below, p. 87.
[9] See below, pp. 125–127.
[10] See especially Chapter Six of *The Significance of the Synoptic Miracles* for my exegetical study of and interpretation of the acts of Jesus.

their most powerful weapon — Death. Quite assured that he was powerless against their ultimate form of attack, they had crucified him. But their strongest weapon was not enough — they overestimated their strength. If they had fully recognized the awesome power of God in Christ, Paul says, they never would have crucified him at all. That is what he literally says in I Cor. 2:8: "None of the rulers of this age understood this; for if they had, they would not have crucified the Lord of glory."

But they did not understand this. They were confident of their superiority, and they had decided to attack Jesus. But in reality, they found themselves attacked, and Jesus emerged victorious over Death. In the resurrection — and this is why the resurrection is the heart of Paul's thought — God rescues Jesus, or, to put it in other terms, the combined strength of God the Father and God the Son prevails over these evil forces. Their worst weapon, Death, is met and mastered in the person of Christ. This is why the resurrection is the vibrant center of Paul's thought, that fulcrum upon which all else rotates and depends. Paul insists, twice in one paragraph, emphatically, unambiguously, and ardently, that the resurrection is the palpitating core of all that he proclaims: "If Christ has not been raised, then our preaching is in vain and your faith is in vain. . . . If Christ has not been raised, your faith is futile and you are still in your sins" (ch. 15:14, 17). For Paul, the issues are as clearly drawn as that. If the resurrection is not factual, Christianity is false, our faith is in vain, Paul's labors are futile, and we are of all men most to be pitied because we have placed our confidence and our hope in the inferior of the two great combatants. But Paul goes on — our hope is not futile because there *is* a resurrection: "But in fact Christ *has been raised* from the dead" (v. 20). The resurrection assumes enormous significance for Paul and for the whole early church,[11] because the resurrection is the affirmation in his-

[11] From this point of view, notice the quotations from The Acts given in Ch. 4, n. 8, above. The early preachers told of the life of Jesus in an

tory, available for all to see, that concretely reveals that God is stronger than even the worst weapon of Satan, Death itself.

To move on, however, we must notice what Paul goes on to call Jesus in v. 20, Jesus is called " the first fruits of those who have fallen asleep." He repeats this title, "the first fruits," in v. 23. What he means by that phrase is that Jesus is the " first fruits," the core, the beginning installment, the first phase of that coming cleansed cosmos which will include man and his physical environment. That new world, that cleansed cosmos which for Jewish apocalyptic lay entirely in the future, was, for Paul, already in existence as of the resurrection, at least in embryonic form. In the resurrection, a part of the cosmos under Satan's control — the body of Jesus — was ripped out of the evil world and exists even now as an entity beyond Satan's grasp. God reached into this world and pulled Jesus out of it. The raised body of Jesus is no longer under the influence of Satan but is instead the first installment, the " first fruits," the even now existing core of that coming creation. That is, again what makes the resurrection so significant to Paul, for it is undeniable historical proof that even as God rescued Jesus, so also God will rescue the balance of the creation — each, however, in its own order, first Jesus, and then at his coming, us (v. 23). But more than just *us:* his coming will release or reveal not only the sons of God, the elect, but the whole creation, the rest of creation which is now languishing under its bondage to decay (Rom. 8:21-23). The new crea-

---

almost matter-of-fact way until they came to the story of the resurrection. At this point, one can almost hear them pause to take a breath and then, speaking of the resurrection, cry out, " of this we are witnesses! " On the resurrection in Paul, Nygren writes: " To Paul the resurrection of Christ is God's mightiest act. It is by this that the new age decisively arrived " (*op. cit.*, p. 48). Compare this to the tendency of Denney to move the emphasis back from the resurrection to the death of Jesus (see Ch. 2, n. 2 above). The difference is due to the fact that Denney rejects demonology (see Ch. 2, n. 2, above), whereas Nygren strongly affirms the motif of sin as slavery under Satan (see Ch. 4, n. 10, above).

tion is already begun in the resurrection. The new cleansed cosmos already has its germinative center — the raised body of Jesus.

And so, according to Paul's thought, the two ages, the two worlds, are coexisting even now. On the one hand, we have the present evil age under the control of the world rulers of this present darkness. We have this body of sin, this evil world, under the control of the evil spirit who reigns as god of this world. But simultaneously, we have the new age, already in existence. And just as the evil age has a spirit over it, so does the new age — but the spirit brooding over and activating the new world is the Holy Spirit. Even as Satan dwells in and controls the evil age, in like manner, the Holy Spirit dwells in and energizes the new world. The Holy Spirit is the spirit of the age to come (Eph. 1:13-14 clearly identifies the Holy Spirit with the future inheritance, and equally obviously, I Cor. 2:12 contrasts the Holy Spirit with the spirit of this age). That future age is already a reality, and the Spirit of that future age is hence also already a reality, even now working, in the body of Christ.

Here we take an important step forward in Paul's thought. Thus far we have been speaking of the two worlds as if they stood side by side but separate. They are distinct entities, one under the evil spirit and the other under the Holy Spirit. But they are not separate. They overlap. They ought to be drawn like this:

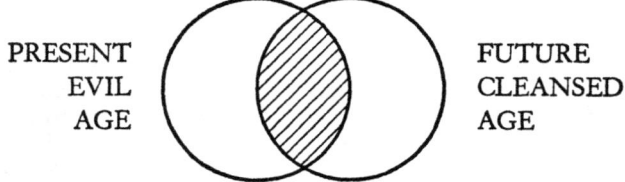

And the church lives in the shaded area. It is the church that lives between the ages (the church " upon whom the end of the

The Church, the New Creation, Salvation 81

ages has come," I Cor. 10:11). It is upon us, the church, that the end of the ages has come. The church lives under the control of both of these spirits, Satan and the Holy Spirit. The Holy Spirit is not spilled out broadside over the whole world in general. Romans 5:5 insists that the Holy Spirit has been given " to us "; ch. 8:11 insists that the Spirit dwells " in you " — members of the elect; v. 14 insists that only the sons of God are led by the Spirit, and Gal. 4:6 has the same idea; II Cor. 1:22 and ch. 5:5 insist that it is " to us," the elect, that the Spirit is given as guarantee; and I Cor. 2:14 flatly insists that the " natural man " does not have the Spirit active in him. The world outside the church is not under the control of the Holy Spirit of God but remains the present evil age with its world rulers of wickedness and its own god. The evil spirits have not been fully and finally defeated and the entire cosmos restored to God's rule.[12] This is why Paul can insist

[12] This, of course, is the view of Oscar Cullmann. In his well-known illustration in which he compares the powers and principalities to creatures now tethered or tied on a leash (*Christ and Time*, p. 193; The Westminster Press, 1951), he maintains that since the resurrection those creatures are no longer enemies of God but reconciled servants carrying out the will of God — or, if not "reconciled servants," at least captive subordinate forces obliged to execute Jesus' will. Hence, Cullmann can go on to write that since the resurrection " *Christ rules over all things in heaven and on earth* " (*op. cit.,* p. 151). Clinton Morrison, however, who studied with Cullmann at Basel, contradicts his teacher at this point in many telling phrases. In *The Powers That Be* (London: SCM Press, Ltd., 1960), p. 53, he writes: " There is no evidence of an early Christian doctrine that these powers are anything but evil and hostile to the church as long as they exist." Again he writes: " The passages referring to Christ's victory and lordship affirm essentially that in Christ believers are no longer subject to the spiritual powers of this world. . . . The decisive event changed the believers' status; they became sons of God. It did not however change the character or impair the effectiveness of the powers for they were yet able to rule . . . and even threaten Christian freedom, Gal. 4:9, Col. 2:20. Far from believing that the powers were subdued or converted, Paul insists that Christians beware of the powers, Col. 2:8, Eph. 6:18 " (pp. 45, 118). And finally Morrison addresses himself to Cullmann directly: " There is no New Testament evidence whatever to confirm the contention that these

that the church is still buffeted and attacked by Satan. Satan is still actively seeking to impede the progress of the church.[13] This is what Luther meant in his two phrases: "Man is a beast of burden, made to be ridden and not always able to choose his own rider"; and *simul iustus et peccator,* at one and the same time a saint and a sinner. We are ridden, attacked, helped, and hindered by supernatural forces. We are at one and the same time a saint, seized and set aside by God in the Spirit, and simultaneously exposed to Satan.

This fact, that the church and only the church is exposed to these two spirits, helps us to understand the otherwise inexplicable fact mentioned earlier in discussing Paul's conversion.[14] It is in his postconversion life, not in his preconversion experiences, that Paul gives evidence of a shattered and divided personality. The subjective view of his conversion claims that before his conversion he was an unhappy, driven man beset by a sense of fear and futility. This does not square with his own views as set forth in Phil., ch. 3. He was aggressive, confident, cocksure of himself, motivated by zeal. He was not a splintered personality, but a cohesive well-knit personality because he had only one ruler, Satan. But once converted, seized by God in Christ, the divided life began. For then he was under the control of two competitive

---

hostile powers were in some way harnessed or 're-commissioned' to a positive responsibility in the kingdom of Christ, and could therefore be called His servants. . . . Rather than appointed servants who have 'lost' their 'evil character,' the New Testament is more inclined to look upon these powers as enslaved, for it considers them hostile until they are finally out of action by Christ's return. Such texts as Rom. 8:38, I Cor. 15:23, and Eph. 6:11 prove Barth, Cullmann, and others to have exceeded the meaning of the New Testament (if not actually opposed to it) in their argument for the positive place of the powers in the kingdom of Christ. . . . That this interpretation of the powers' conscription to serve in the kingdom of Christ is foreign to the New Testament is apparent in the total lack of evidence to support it" (pp. 45–46).

[13] See below, pp. 83–85.
[14] See above, p. 42.

The Church, the New Creation, Salvation

forces: the Holy Spirit that had grasped him and the evil spirit that sought to win him back. This is why Paul must insist in Rom., ch. 7, that it is he, Paul the Christian, who finds a war going on in himself (v. 23), and why he must proclaim himself a wretched man at odds with himself (v. 24). The same imagery of warfare is seen in Gal. 5:17.[15] One could cite as evidence, also, the otherwise astounding paradox of language in I Thess. 1:6: "You received the word in *much affliction, with joy* inspired by the Holy Spirit."

But even though this struggle goes on, there is, nonetheless, this exuberant note of confidence, of victory. There is a shout of triumph that wells up out of the continuing struggle because Paul knows that nothing in all of creation can separate him from the love of God. He understands the significance of the resurrection. The resurrection is proof that the worst weapon of Satan is insufficient; God's superiority is a historical fact. Jesus is stronger; death has lost its potency. Thus, even though still attacked, still exposed, Paul can shout out that the victory is already his (Rom. 7:25).[16] In I Cor. 15:57, precisely this same juxtaposition of triumph and defeat — or better, triumph in defeat — is present. This is the full meaning of those places where Paul calls the Holy Spirit the *guarantee* of our salvation (Eph. 1:14; II Cor. 1:22).

The point that ought to come through clearly in this discussion

---

[15] The only difference in the Romans and Galatians passages is that in Romans, the enemy who wars against the Christian is the law that is in the hands of the enemy (see Ch. 3, n. 2, above), whereas in Galatians the enemy is "the flesh." But as J. A. T. Robinson has pointed out, the flesh is not to be interpreted in a Greek flesh-spirit dualistic sense. Instead, to be in the flesh means to be under the control of evil spirits who work in and through the flesh: "To be in the flesh is to be subject to the powers that control it. . . . It is that (*sarx*) by virtue of which the powers have their grip over us" (*op. cit.*, p. 22).

[16] This verse is exactly where it belongs — a cry of triumph in the midst of wretchedness. If it were not there, we would have to assume that "the amanuensis got confused"! (See Ch. 3, n. 3, above.)

has already been said, namely, that the resurrection of Jesus did not end the tyranny of the devil, not even as far as the church is concerned. The church, rather than being freed from the devil and beyond his range, is still exposed to him. As a matter of fact, the church stands especially exposed to him to a degree even greater than the rest of the world outside the church, for the devil sees that he is in danger of losing those who belong to the church and thus it is against the church that his most violent attacks are turned. This is what accounts for the logic of Paul as evidenced in his epistles. One extended example will illustrate the point. The Corinthian congregation had come to be divided, split into factions and cliques. Among those cliques were those who had come to look upon Paul as an inferior apostle, second rate, no equal to either the preaching of Apollos or the authority of Peter, who had been with the Lord. Hence, there were groups that rejected Paul and were of Peter's party or the party of Apollos (I Cor. 1:12). In short, Paul's apostleship is under fire, and his authority is being rejected. He is accused of weakness (II Cor. 10:10). In a blistering and emotional self-defense, Paul, in the last four chapters of II Corinthians, tries to make it clear that he is truly an apostle. As proof of this, he writes II Cor., chs. 11 and 12. In those two chapters he lists example after example of the sufferings he has undergone. In ch. 11:24 ff., he says: " Five times I have received . . . forty lashes less one. Three times I have been beaten with rods; once I was stoned. Three times I have been shipwrecked; a night and a day I have been adrift at sea; . . . in danger from rivers, danger from robbers, danger from my own people, danger from Gentiles, danger in the city, danger in the wilderness, danger at sea, danger from false brethren; in toil and hardship, through many a sleepless night, in hunger and thirst, often without food, in cold and exposure." And he further insists that these obstacles he has met are traceable in one form or another to the activity of Satan. These hin-

The Church, the New Creation, Salvation

drances are being perpetrated through false workmen, servants of Satan (vs. 13-15). Then, in ch. 12, he goes on in the same vein, becoming even more intimate and personal, telling that he had been afflicted by sickness which hindered his work, and that he had pleaded with God to see that he be released from this thorn in the flesh, but his prayer had not been answered. Instead, all the days of his life he was attacked by what he himself defined as an angel of Satan sent to harass him (v. 7).

Now, this is an astounding argument when analyzed critically. Paul is accused of being a weak person (ch. 10:10), and as proof of his true apostleship, he confesses the very thing he is accused of — weakness, impotency (ch. 11:6)! He tells that he has been beaten from pillar to post, harassed by sickness, attacked by servants of Satan, his back laid bare by the lash of the law, kicked and stoned across all Asia Minor, left to die in the wilderness. And *these* are the proofs of his true apostleship, evidence of the fact that Jesus of Nazareth is truly active in him! It is an incredible argument! But what is more incredible, it carries the day! Subsequent events show that the Corinthians accept the logic and are reconciled to him and accept him anew as their father in the faith, a true apostle. Now, this kind of logic and its success is possible only when one recognizes the world view and the orientation that the early Christians had toward suffering. They recognized Satan as a still active force, resisting God. They further recognized, therefore, that anyone who identified himself with God and was being mightily used by God would consequently be subject to the counterattack of the devil. The devil would see in the servant of Christ a foe, and would therefore do all in his power to defeat that foe and nullify his effectiveness.[17] Hence,

[17] Paul does not even hesitate to state the reverse negative corollary, namely, that the perverters of the gospel and those who oppose Paul are perverting and opposing precisely to avoid this Satanic attack. Schweitzer, writing on Gal. 6:12, says: "Paul refuses to admit that the Jewish zealots are acting only because they are deceived. He holds that they are also

in a very real way, a man's true discipleship becomes evidenced in his suffering. The more fully a man is used of God, the more exposed he is to Satanic attack. Jesus himself is the prime example of this pattern — he who was God's own prime representative was attacked by the powers of this age and crucified.[18] Great

---

moved by fear. They see in his own case what those who, by preaching the pure doctrine of the cross, interfere with the plans of the angels, have to endure in the way of persecution and suffering. This they desire to escape. That is why they set up the law alongside the cross" (*Mysticism*, p. 200).

[18] This is the direct opposite of the view of official Judaism, which had abandoned the apocalyptic or Danielic view of tribulation as arising in God-opposing forces and not in God (see Schweitzer's comment, Ch. 2, n. 1, above), and had returned anew to the Old Testament principle of retribution — the view that the good are blessed by God here and now and the evil immediately punished by God. There was consequently no doctrine of a suffering servant in official Judaism. On this point Cullmann writes (*The Christology of the New Testament*, p. 58; The Westminster Press, rev. ed., 1964): "Even if it were possible to find the Judaism of the New Testament period the conception of an eschatological saviour of Israel who consciously assumes the role of the *ebed Yahweh*, it would be a conviction which arose on the periphery of Judaism. The thought that the Messiah had to suffer is foreign to the official expectation at least." To bulwark this observation, Cullmann presents, in the two pages that follow that remark, a summary of the Targum exegesis of the suffering servant passages and concludes that the Targum work "twists the text to mean just the opposite of what it says" (p. 59). (Davies says substantially the same thing, *op. cit.*, p. 277.) Instead of seeing a servant of God as suffering, official Judaism, by the principle of retribution, saw him as triumphing. It was held that God would reward — not punish — the righteous, and this is why the Pharisees despised the demoniacs as supremely evil, and why they refused to help the injured — to aid such as that would be to oppose the will of God who had struck them down in the first place. Jesus, on the other hand, looks upon the demoniacs, not as supremely evil persons who have sold themselves to the devil, but as supremely unfortunate people who have been overwhelmed against their will. In like manner, Jesus, instead of shunning the injured, commands men to aid them in his parable of the good Samaritan. It is because official Judaism had abandoned apocalyptic views and returned to the principle of retribution that the Jew could not accept Jesus as Messiah. His suffering on the cross proved, to the average Jew, that Jesus was a blasphemer, punished by God.

suffering was a proof of great service — God was active in that person. Hence Paul could cry out, "I consider that the sufferings of this present time are not worth comparing with the glory that is to be revealed to us" (Rom. 8:18). He could rejoice in those sufferings, not in the sense of seeing them as good or purgative, a cleansing chastisement sent of God, but rather, in the sense that in their own way they proved that he was effectively being used of God, and consequently being counterattacked by Satan, who was seeking to impede or end his effectiveness. Paul was no masochistic idiot who delighted in rocks bounding off his back — he did not call suffering good.[19] But those attacks proved both to him and to the Corinthians that he was a true apostle, being used by God, and thus being resisted by Satan.

This brings us back to the Col. 2:15 passage. We have already noted that some theologians interpret this passage to mean exactly the opposite of what we have been claiming. In short, they argue that as of the cross-resurrection, the resistance of the cosmic foes has ended.[20] All celestial resistance has ended as of the empty tomb and crucifixion, for that was a time when Jesus "*disarmed* the principalities and powers." Such is not Paul's view. The suffering of the church is evidence enough against that. But, more than that, this Col. 2:15 verse just does not allow such an interpretation. The participle *apekdusamenos* of Col. 2:15 does not mean "to disarm," but rather, "to strip off" or "free oneself

---

This is why Paul insists that the suffering of Jesus on the cross was a "stumbling block" to the Jew (I Cor. 1:23).

[19] We must reject out of hand the words of Quell as he comments on Matt. 24:10 f. (Kittel, *op. cit.*, "Love," p. 46): "These words make it clear what it means to love God. It means glowing with passion for God, the passionate eagerness to suffer that characterizes the little flock." The early church, Paul included, did *not* desire suffering — suffering was evil, of Satan. But when that suffering did come, it was rejoiced in as evidence that one had been espied by Satan, even as Jesus had, as a servant of God, and was thus fair game for attack.

[20] See Cullmann's view, note 12 of this chapter.

from," or "disrobe oneself" (this is the *only* way in which Paul ever uses the word; see ch. 3:9 and the use of the noun in ch. 2:11). What the Greek literally says is not that Jesus disarmed these powers, nor does it even say that he stripped them or disrobed them (that is the interpretation given by Taylor, but it will not stand up linguistically, for such an interpretation would demand that the participle be active, with the principalities as object, but the participle is in the middle form).[21] The verb form is reflexive. Jesus has stripped himself free — not stripping them, but himself. He has freed himself of their power. They continue to be active — but not against him. Over him, their hold is ended. He personally is free of them. His resurrected body is beyond their reach. They can and do still attack the church and temporarily appear to prevail against it, but Jesus himself they cannot touch. That is the significance of Phil. 2:10-11, in which it says that every knee *will* bow before Jesus. It is a future tense in both instances. Paul actually breaks Greek grammatical rules to make this clear. The fact that the accepted text has the subjunctive forms *kampsēi* and *exomologēsētai* conceals this fact, for, of course, depending on the interpretation that one wishes to give, the aorist subjunctive can be looked upon as either a future reality or something already begun. But the oldest texts do *not* have the subjunctive, which they ought to have in a *hina* clause, but they have the future tense instead.[22] This is precisely that violation of grammatical rules which Paul is capable of entering into when he wishes to avoid being misunderstood. It is in the future that the foe will be subjugated. The resurrection reveals Jesus as superior, but it has not ended resistance. Thus, since their resistance is not yet ended, and because Jesus himself is beyond their reach, these evil powers vent their rage on the only object

[21] Taylor gives this interpretation in *Atonement*, p. 92.
[22] In *Christ the Conqueror* (London: S.P.C.K., 1954), p. 114, Ragnar Leivestad writes: "Most of the mss read *exomologēsētai* (future) in Phil. 2:11, . . . thus denoting that the event is expected to take place in the future."

The Church, the New Creation, Salvation

of hatred within their reach, the body of Christ, and the church is thus exposed to the "principalities and powers" seeking to separate it from the love of God (Rom. 8:35 f.).

It is at this point that the true significance of the Parousia can be seen in Paul's thought. It is then, only in the future, at Christ's return, that the devil and all his weapons will be finally stilled. Paul makes this clear not only in his earliest epistles when he tells us that it will be at Jesus' coming that the enemies will be destroyed by the breath of his mouth (II Thess. 2:8 f.), but he insists upon this same truth all through his epistles. In I Cor., ch. 15, Paul has insisted that the resurrection of Jesus is a fact, and that therefore death has been deprived of its abiding significance. Death has, he shouts, already lost its potency, and thus he can exult, "Death is swallowed up in victory. O death, where is thy victory? O death, where is thy sting?" (I Cor. 15:54-55). And yet, death still continues as a fact. Beaten in principle, revealed as inferior, yet it continues on in fact.[23] There are no histories of rapture in the early church. All die. And it will not be until the coming of Jesus that death and the great cosmic host is destroyed. In one of his last epistles, in imagery strikingly familiar to imagery he used in his earliest epistles — cf. I Thess. 5:8; Eph. 6:14-17 — Paul must caution against the continued "wiles of the devil" (Eph. 6:11). In I Cor. 15:24, Paul speaks of the end, the coming of Jesus, and in v. 25 of the putting underfoot of the still-active enemies.[24] It is only then, in the future, that the fact of death will be conquered.

[23] Leivestad writes: "If the cosmic rulers have in principle been dethroned at the resurrection of Christ, they continue to exercise authority as long as the old cosmos has not been succeeded by the new" (*op. cit.,* p. 96). Again, he writes: "In Christ, they [the believers] are new creatures belonging to the age of the resurrection, but as long as they are in the body they are subject to the conditions of this world. . . . It is true that Christ proved Himself victorious over death in His resurrection, but death was not abolished then, not even for the believers" (p. 127).

[24] Even Cullmann is forced to recognize that in I Cor. 15:25, Paul recognizes the evil forces as still evil and still active until the return of

It is for this reason that the early church looked not only backward in rejoicing to the resurrection but also forward with even more rejoicing to the Parousia. The resurrection was proof that God was stronger than Satan, and that the return of Jesus would be the culmination or manifestation of that superiority, the end of all resistance, the rescue of the church out from under the hand of the great adversary. The burning hope of the imminent Parousia was the characteristic hallmark of the early Christian community. Eschatology was the heart of its hope because demonology was the base of its world view.

Oscar Cullmann's well-known illustration of the turning point of a war is still perhaps the best way of illustrating the relationship between the resurrection and the return. Every war has a critical turning point, a decisive battle that puts the end out of doubt. For example, in World War II, once Hitler's counteroffensive in Belgium, the Battle of the Bulge, was turned back, the outcome of the war in Europe was out of all doubt. The spinal column of Nazi forces was cracked, and it was impossible for Germany to win. Yet the war dragged on. Men fought and died, and those on the eventual winning side were still exposed to the enemy. Though their side was guaranteed triumph, they were still under fire. Precisely the same thing took place in the resurrection. It was the turning point. It was the personal victory of Jesus that assured God's superiority. It was evidence that the worst of the enemy had been used and found wanting. And yet, in waiting for the final end, those on God's side still suffered. This is what accounts for the otherwise inexplicable attitude of ambiguity that characterized the early church. They rejoiced in a victory that was already theirs. They were convinced that they were on the winning side, and yet to those outside the church, they were of all men most to be pitied. For it was in the church

---

Jesus. He refers to the passage as "an apparent contradiction" (*Christology*, p. 224).

The Church, the New Creation, Salvation

that they came to be battered and beaten, abused and apparently destroyed. But rising up out of their apparent defeat was the cry of victory. The church is the absolute paradox. It is victorious in apparent defeat. Beaten, Christians rise again. Thrown down, they will be raised up in triumph. But each in his own order. First Christ was cast down and then lifted up; at his coming the church, his body, now thrown down, will be lifted up.

CHAPTER 6

Paul's View of the Body of Christ, Baptism, and the Holy Spirit

Two THINGS have already been said to which we now return: (1) we have insisted that the raised body of Christ was itself the firstfruits of the coming cleansed cosmos; and (2) we have insisted that the Christian, here in this world, is already identified with that new age, under the control of the Holy Spirit, who is the ruler of the age to come. In this chapter these two ideas are developed further. This must be done in a circuitous and apparently nonconnected way.

We begin by recalling that Deissmann tells us that one of the characteristic phrases of Paul — indeed, his hallmark in Deissmann's eye — is "in Christ," with its corresponding corollary "Christ in me." Thus the Christian is in Christ and Christ is in the Christian in a way to be defined. Furthermore, and in line with this, when Paul speaks of the church he prefers another word to that of "church." He uses the word "church" approximately fifty times, but almost twice that often, over eighty times, he prefers to use the term "body." The church is the body of Christ. In both instances, then, whether he is speaking of the individual or whether he is speaking of the plurality of saints, Paul's language gravitates to this idea of seeing Christians as "in Christ," as parts of the "body of Christ."

The question, then, that must be asked, is this: How does Paul understand that phrase "in Christ"? Is it objective, physical, an

The Body, Baptism, the Spirit

organic relationship? Or is it subjective, emotional, mystical, or moral? Is the Christian literally and physically attached to Jesus? Or is "in Christ" a term to be understood instead in psychological rather than biological terms? The same type of questions can be asked of the companion term, "the body of Christ." When Paul speaks of the church as the body of Christ, does he use the term symbolically or literally? Does he mean that body or group of believers who identify themselves with the goal of Jesus? That is, does he see two numerically distinct entities — over here, Jesus; and over there, that group which exists as a collective body that has adopted his point of view and believes in him? Or does Paul literally mean that the church is the physical organic body of Jesus, his arms and legs and eyes?

The answer is uncomfortable but unmistakable.[1] It is uncomfortable because the temper of our times is existential, subjective, spiritualized, psychological. We would prefer to see these ties between Jesus and the individual or between Jesus and the church in moral rather than in metaphysical terms. But Paul goes counter to his whole usual manner of expression here and insists upon using language that is so concrete and physical, so nonspiritualized, that it falls on our ears with an almost jarring harshness. We have already noted that Paul's mind ordinarily goes from the concrete to the abstract, regularly leaving behind him the specifics and moving into generalized discussions of intangible verities.[2] He does this regularly, *except* when he speaks of being in Christ or

---

[1] Even Kennedy, who has no personal appreciation of the idea, is obliged to acknowledge what is the primary direction of Paul's language: "The formula *en kristoi* constructed by Paul characterizes the relation of Christian to Jesus Christ as an existence in the pneumatic Christ to be conceived locally. . . . The question whether we have to take the local idea, which is the basis of the formula, in its proper sense or merely as a metaphorical formula, cannot be decided with a high degree of certainty, yet the former alternative has the higher degree of probability" (*op. cit.*, pp. 120–121).

[2] See above, p. 20.

of the body of Christ. Here, Paul reverses himself and uses imagery that is strikingly concrete and physical. This is seen very clearly, for example, when he begins to discuss the nature of the church as the body of Christ in I Cor., ch. 12. He speaks of the body, not in corporate or in communal terms, but rather, in corporal terms, the true physical body of Jesus. He goes so far as to insist that some Christians are the actual hands and feet of Jesus (v. 15) and others are organs of the senses, one an eye, another an ear (vs. 17, 21). This same idea continues all through the extended paragraph. In vs. 23 f. some Christians are lesser organs of the body, private parts, to be treated with great modesty, inferior parts not to be exposed, whereas others are the higher organs. But in all cases the Christians are described as real limbs of Jesus, actual physical members of one concrete body. Paul seems to be saying that the church is the ongoing incarnation.[3] In a very real way, the church is not separate from Jesus, a group that shares his goals but is numerically distinct, but instead, the church is the actual flesh of Jesus — that body through which he is still active in the world. Even as he was truly physically present in the body out of Mary's womb, even so now he is truly physically present in this new body, the church, the ongoing incarnation.

This idea of a physical tie between Jesus and the believer is perhaps even more strikingly seen in the terminology of "in Christ." Here again the meaning is unmistakably physical or local, rather than moral or symbolic. The Christian is physically and organically tied to Jesus. Christ seems to be understood as a realm of

[3] J. A. T. Robinson writes: "Our contention is that his [Paul's] doctrine of the resurrection body of Christ, under all its forms is a direct extension of his understanding of the incarnation" (*op. cit.*, p. 56). And again: "*The appearance on which Paul's whole faith and apostleship was founded was the revelation of the resurrection body of Christ, not as an individual, but as the Christian community.* . . . Since that day, when he saw Christ in the church he was persecuting, it seems he can no longer look into the eyes of a Christian without meeting there the gaze of Christ!" (p. 58).

The Body, Baptism, the Spirit

a living physical organism into which the individual Christian is grafted, becoming physically united to Jesus. For example, in Gal. 4:19 the Revised Standard Version is so polite that we can almost miss the blunt physical terminology that is involved. What Paul is literally saying is that he is suffering the pangs of pregnancy and birth with the wayward Galatians, suffering until the embryo of Jesus be formed in them, that is, until they in turn become pregnant with Jesus — the Greek literally says "until they get filled up" with Jesus. Here we have one of those typical Pauline mélanges. He gets his imagery all mixed up. First he says he is in labor pains, but in the same sentence he says that he is in labor pains for "my little children" — people already born! Then he closes the sentence by hoping that they, no longer he, might become pregnant with Jesus. But though he mixes the metaphor, the cast of his language is unmistakable. It is crassly physical, and that is what is striking in the light of the tendency we have noted — his tendency to move away from specific terminology to abstract.

Galatians 4:19 is one such passage; Gal. 2:20 is another. He says, "It is no longer I who live, but Christ who lives in me." The same idea of a physical tie between Jesus and Paul is seen also in Gal. 6:17 and Col. 1:24. The tie that exists between Jesus and Paul is so real and physical that when Paul is being beaten, Jesus himself is actually present and suffering. The same idea of a physical relationship is perhaps put out of all doubt when Paul actually uses the language of sexual intercourse to illustrate the tie that exists between Jesus and the church. Unfortunately the intimacy of this relationship and its physical description here also are lost in our refined translations.[4] The same idea of a

---

[4] J. A. T. Robinson writes: "It is to be noted how uncompromisingly physical is the language in which Paul depicts Christians as going to compose the body of Christ. . . . This is particularly clear in . . . Romans (7.4). . . . The unity is much closer than the English words would suggest. For the metaphor, as the context shows, is one of sexual union, and

physical relationship between Jesus and the church is seen in Rom. 6:5, where Paul is speaking of Baptism. He insists that in Baptism we are literally " grown together " (*symphytoi*) with Jesus, in the same way that a branch is grafted into and organically united to the tree into which it is placed. Again and again and again, both in major concepts and in minor terms, this idea of a physical union between Jesus and the believer appears in Paul's letters. For example, Paul does not content himself with saying in Eph. 5:30 that Christians are "members " of the body of Christ, but instead he goes on in Col. 2:19 to use joltingly physical language, insisting that we are " membranes, ligaments, joints " in the body of Christ.

Perhaps the most astounding bit of evidence in this respect is one of the conclusions Paul draws from this way of thinking. So thoroughly is he convinced of the individual Christian's tie to Jesus that he insists that the tie has implications for those around the Christian. In I Cor., ch. 7, Paul is answering questions asked of him concerning divorce. It has been asked, Should a Christian woman divorce a non-Christian man? And his answer is that, under the circumstances made known to him, no, that should not be done. But the logic by which he comes to this conclusion is astounding. He argues that since the woman is a Christian she is therefore physically united to Jesus. And since she is married, she is physically united to her husband. Therefore, like links in a chain, this nonbelieving husband, by means of the connection

---

its presupposition is that the relationship of Christians to Christ is that of 'one flesh' (*cf.* Eph. 5.28-32): they are fused in a single basar " (*op. cit.,* p. 52). Schweitzer also comments on these verses: " Paul does not hesitate to use the same word — *kollasthai,* cleave, derived from Gen. 2:24 — of bodily union between man and woman, and union with Christ " (*Mysticism,* p. 127). This is what leads Schweitzer to conclude: " The mystical body of Christ is thus for Paul not a pictorial expression, nor a conception which has arisen out of symbolic and ethical reflections, but an actual entity, . . . an actual physical union between Christ and the Elect. . . . The Elect and Christ partake in the same corporeity " (pp. 127, 121).

The Body, Baptism, the Spirit

he has with his wife, is by extension physically united to Jesus through that wife! In this section, I Cor. 7:12-14, not one word is said about the husband having faith or any other subjective attitude toward Jesus. On the contrary, it is specifically affirmed that he is a non-Christian — and yet Paul uses exactly the same word for him, "made clean, sanctified" (*hegiastai*), that he uses for Christians.[5] And even with that, Paul is not finished! He goes on to insist, in v. 14b, that even the children, because they are physically part of her, are purified because of her contact with Jesus.

I will not even argue back when it is said that these verses are difficult — nearly impossibly — to live with. But that is what they say, whether we like them or not, and it does show how realistically and fully Paul accepts this idea of the Christian's being

---

[5] On this verse, Schweitzer writes: "The unbelieving partner, through bodily connection with the believing, has a share in the latter's being-in-Christ and thereby becomes with him a member of the community of the sanctified. . . . This verse shows that Paul is prepared to accept in the fullest measure the implications of his doctrine of believers with Christ as a bodily union" (*Mysticism*, p. 128). Schweitzer is not alone in this understanding of the passage. Nock writes: "Exactly the same quasi-physical notion is implied in the argument against divorcing a non-Christian partner in marriage: I Cor. 7:14. . . . The physical union of man and woman can transfer something of the saving corporality of Christ" (*op. cit.*, p. 150). C. A. Anderson Scott also insists that Paul approves the continuance of the mixed marriage because in a real way the unbelieving partner is actually consecrated or made holy. He writes that the marriage "holds him or her [the non-Christian mate] in some sense and in some degree dedicated to God and so in closer touch than otherwise with the Divine grace" (*op. cit.*, p. 221). The only way in which Scott and Nock differ from Schweitzer and Paul is in their attempt to limit this "making holy." Nock insists that "something" of the saving corporality is transferred — there is no such qualifying diminutive in Paul. Scott tries to give the passage an internalized twist by saying that "in some sense and in some degree" the individual becomes "dedicated to God" and "in closer touch with grace." Such limitations are not found in Paul — the passage, on the contrary, flatly maintains that the mate is *unbelieving* and is *nonetheless* made holy, sanctified, as fully as any Christian.

physically in Christ, literally a part of the physical body of Jesus. This argument from the physical, against divorce, is the same argument he employs in denouncing going in to a prostitute (ch. 6:16). The Christian male is physically united to Jesus. Thus to have intercourse with a prostitute is not simply to soil himself but also to drag Jesus into this degrading relationship: "Shall I therefore take the members of Christ and make them members of a prostitute? Never!"[6] I repeat, it is granted without argument that these are indeed difficult passages to apply in our day. But I would insist that if a person is willing to accept them, he is forced to see how they fit into Paul's overall thought. We have already seen how Paul looks upon the raised body of Christ as the physical core of the coming cleansed cosmos, the "firstfruits" of the new world.[7] Since this is a physical cosmos, Paul finds himself obliged to use physical terminology when he speaks of the Christian's being part of that future cosmos. It is a physical cosmos; thus the tie to it must be physical. We are physically tied to Jesus, physically united to that future realm. The raised body of Jesus is the place free of Satan's power, the place where the

[6] On this verse, Schweitzer writes: "Intercourse with a harlot is ruinous, because thereby a union is established which necessarily annuls the previous union with Christ" (*Mysticism*, p. 128). Robinson also sees this verse as evidence of Paul's corporal conception of the body of Christ. (*Op. cit.*, p. 52.) Robinson continues: "To say that individuals are members of a person is indeed a very violent use of language — and the context shows that Paul obviously meant it to be violent. . . . But . . . when Paul applied it [the term "body"] to the Church, . . . it . . . conveyed *not corporate but corporal*. . . . One must be chary of speaking of the 'metaphor' of the body of Christ. . . . They are in literal fact the risen organism of Christ's person in all its concrete reality" (pp. 50–51). Nock writes: "What is the meaning of this recurrent *in Christ Jesus?* . . . This is no metaphor; it describes what Paul believes to be literal fact. In I Corinthians he constantly uses it, not as a figure of speech, but as the basis of arguments, as for instance in 1:13 apropos of their factions, 'Is Christ divided?' Consider above all 6:15-17" (*op. cit.*, p. 150).

[7] See above, pp. 78–79.

The Body, Baptism, the Spirit

Holy Spirit dwells. Thus when we are physically in Christ, we are under the Spirit's rule. This is why Paul can use the two phrases "in Christ" and "in the Spirit" interchangeably.[8] If one is in Christ, he is by definition tied to that physical realm where the Spirit dwells.[9]

Furthermore, we have already said that Jesus is beyond the range of Satan's power.[10] Yet Paul sees Jesus as suffering with him right there and then (Gal. 6:17; Col. 1:24). In short, Paul is ambiguous. Jesus is beyond Satan's power, out of this world, and yet exposed to Satan, in this world in his body the church, still attacked. This fits in perfectly with what we have said about the church's living between the ages. There is an area of overlap.[11] The church is identified with both ages, under both Spirits, Satan and the Holy Spirit. One could almost say that the Christian has two bodies: the body of sin, and the body of Christ. Thus Paul can say, "It is no longer I that do it, but sin which dwells within me," while he can simultaneously say, "It is no longer I who live, but Christ who lives in me." The Christian has two bodies. In precisely the same way, Jesus has two bodies. He is

---

[8] Deissmann wrote: "The living Christ is the pneuma. . . . The formula 'in the Spirit' which occurs only 19 times in the Pauline writings is in almost all these places connected with the same specifically Pauline fundamental ideas which elsewhere he connects with the formula 'in Christ'" (*op. cit.*, p. 138). Davies also remarks that "the Christian who is *en kristoi* . . . can also be described in parallel fashion as being *en pneumati*" (*op. cit.*, p. 177). Scott goes on to draw out the fact that in both instances, in Christ or in the Spirit, Paul's mind seems to move in concrete terms of a realm rather than spiritualized terms of a point of view: "Christ is conceived of as in some sense the habitation or dwelling place of the Christian. Like the Spirit He is conceived of as a sphere or atmosphere within which men may live and move" (*op. cit.*, p. 153).

[9] How man enters into that realm, and what the Spirit does in and through man once he has arrived in that realm, is the subject matter of the rest of this chapter. Hence we can drop this line of development at this moment.

[10] See above, pp. 76–77.

[11] See above, the chart, p. 80.

both in the world, exposed to Satan, in the church, and beyond Satan, beyond the world, freed of Satan's power. This is perhaps why the language of sexual intercourse is so exceedingly appropriate. Even as a married couple are two and yet really one, so also Jesus has two bodies, two and yet one. He is united with the church, his bride, sharing her agonies in the present, suffering when one of his limbs is abused, and yet the consummation lies off in the future, when he will return to claim his bride. And thus we see that, via different imagery, we return to the ambiguous idea of a victory won and yet a war continuing, which we saw in discussing the relationship of the resurrection and the Parousia.[12]

If being in Christ is a physical tie, how does it come about? What act ties us to Jesus? We must again take a roundabout route in looking for the answer to this. Not only does Paul speak of being "in Christ" but also he speaks of "faith." Indeed, these two phrases are often combined into one phrase: "faith in Christ." One could therefore speak of a "faith union" that exists between Jesus and the individual.[13] Most commentators take this to mean that it is our faith, our personal response or commitment, that ties us to Jesus.[14] That is, the faith union is

[12] See above, p. 89.

[13] This is a favorite term with Vincent Taylor, and he even entitles one of the subchapters of his work "Faith-Union with the Crucified."

[14] Taylor writes: "This faith arises within man and is the expression of his will" (*Atonement*, p. 136). In *The Gospel According to St. Paul* (Longmans, Green & Company, 1907), p. 60, William DuBose writes: "The only possible . . . redemption for a personal spirit from sin is through its own conquest of sin. The conquest cannot be made for us, but only by us. . . . The power of God to save us actually saves us only as it is made our power to save ourselves." He continues: "In the exercise of his personal endowments of reason and freedom, he constructs himself, he molds himself and shapes his life, his character, his destiny" (p. 264). But DuBose can bring forth no Pauline justification for such views — Rom. 7:15 ff., the references to predestination, and the emphasis upon faith as a gift all deny such freedom of man. Nygren is far closer to Paul when he

The Body, Baptism, the Spirit

seen in subjective or moral terms. We make a decision for Christ, identifying ourselves with him. It is our faith in him that unites us to him. *For this point of view, not one single verse in the entire collection of Pauline epistles can be mustered as support.* Never does Paul say that this union with Jesus is the consequence of faith. On the contrary, Paul makes it exceedingly clear that faith in Christ follows rather than precedes or establishes this relationship. Faith is a consequence, not a cause, of being in Christ.

Paul makes it quite clear that the place where the Christian is joined to Christ, or comes to be in Christ, is not the moment of faith at all — but it is the moment of baptism.[15] That is why

---

writes: "Entirely without our doing, God has placed us in a new situation.... As far as faith is concerned, the meaning is not that affirmations about the gospel are held to be true, but rather that men are gripped and constrained by God's power, and thereby borne into the new age, into life with Christ.... It is not enough to say that the gospel treats of God's power; it is itself the power of God, God's *dunameis*. Whenever the gospel is preached, the power of God is effective unto salvation. The gospel is not the presentation of an idea but the operation of a power snatching men from the powers of destruction.... Faith is only another word for the fact that one belongs to Christ" (*op. cit.*, pp. 154, 78, 67, and 71. See also his many other references to the same effect, namely, that faith is not to be seen in subjective terms as a response of man but in objective terms as an intervention of God — pp. 18, 25, 56, 58, 70, 152, 204, *et al.*). Even Bultmann recognizes that "the New Testament affirms the total incapacity of man to release himself."

[15] Deissmann would disagree with this. He writes: "The assertion that according to Paul baptism is the means of access to Christ, I hold to be incorrect. There are passages which, taken in isolation, can be made to prove it" (*op. cit.*, p. 145). Schweitzer addresses himself directly to Deissmann: "That Paul should have regarded baptism and the Lord's Supper as inherently efficacious acts, and redemption as being bound up with them seems to us inconsistent with the deep spirituality which is elsewhere the shining characteristic of his religion.... Deissmann takes the desperate course of denying its recognition.... Paul simply asserts that it is with baptism that the being-in-Christ and the dying and rising again ... have their beginning in baptism. The idea that it is only through a believing self-surrender to absorption in Christ that the Elect can bring about the mystical fellowship with Him is quite outside of Paul's horizon. He as-

Paul has such a powerful view of baptism, for it is that act which joins a man to Jesus.[16] There is no possibility of mistaking Paul's meaning and intent at this point. We may not like his strongly sacramental emphasis, but that it is there cannot be doubted. "For as many of you as were baptized into Christ have put on

sumes as self-evident that a grafting into Christ takes place in baptism and is bound up with this ceremonial act" (*Mysticism*, pp. 18–19). Deissmann is not the only one who takes the "desperate course of denying its recognition." Davies too protests: "Grotesque . . . the mechanical conception of the Christian life it involves does not do justice to the centrality of Faith in Paul. . . . Nor was it by any celebration of outward rites such as Baptism or the Eucharist that the union and dying and rising with Christ was achieved. . . . On the contrary, it was by faith" (*op. cit.*, pp. 98, 91). Davies' argument would be immeasurably stronger if he could bring forth even one verse of Paul which indicates that it is faith that initiates and establishes this union with Jesus. There is no such verse. Kennedy takes up the same line as Davies: "No statement in the epistles suggests that he looked on baptism as the originating cause of faith. . . . Even the utterance of Gal. 3:27 . . . in no way conflicts with the clear teaching of the entire epistle that faith is primary. For the whole context shows that in this passage faith is the presupposition of baptism" (*op. cit.*, p. 151). The argument just will not stand up against the linguistic evidence. Galatians 3:27 clearly states that it is in baptism that we are united to Christ.

[16] Dibelius writes: "Paul saw in baptism a divine action on human beings, making what God has done in Christ a personal reality to the individual believer, conveying to him at the same time the gift of the Holy Spirit, and so receiving him into the new community of salvation, the body of Christ" (*op. cit.*, p. 121). (Dibelius' remark that baptism also puts a man under the control of the Holy Spirit is affirmed by Cullmann: "Baptism . . . mediates the Holy Spirit" [*Christ and Time*, p. 222]. This insistence that after baptism man is under the Spirit comes to have profound importance for that which follows.) Schweitzer too recognizes the naked sacramental character of Paul's thought: "Being-in-Christ is not a subjective experience brought about by a special effort of faith on the part of the believer, but something which happens in him as in others, in baptism" (*Mysticism*, p. 260). Even Bultmann recognizes this truth: "Baptism is an objective occurrence which happens to the baptized, not simply a symbol for a subjective process within him. Whatever inward experiences the one being baptized may have, Paul does not reflect on them" (*op. cit.*, p. 312).

The Body, Baptism, the Spirit

Christ." (Gal. 3:27.) [17] He says exactly the same thing in Rom. 6:3, 5: "You were baptized into Christ," he begins, and goes on to expand his meaning. We were united to Jesus in baptism, grown together with him in this act like a grafted branch growing into a tree (it is here that Paul uses the word *symphytoi* quoted earlier). Baptism, then, for Paul, is not an act of man in which he consecrates himself unto God. Baptism is instead an act of God. It is God who is active in baptism, active through the church, grasping men to himself and uniting them to Jesus in precisely the same way that the first body of Jesus out of Mary's womb joined men to himself by striding out to the seashore and into the marketplace, choosing men, commanding them to follow, and announcing that they had not chosen him, but that he had chosen them.

As a matter of fact, Paul stresses this idea of God as being the actor in baptism, grasping men and uniting them to Jesus, to such an enormous extent that the Corinthians actually go to an extreme and start baptizing dead people. They reason that if God is the real actor and the efficacy of the act is found, not in the faith of the baptized, but in the power of God, then he can even rescue dead people. Although this is a perversion of Paul's thought,[18] we can see how such a perversion could grow normally out of Paul's strong sacramental view.[19]

---

[17] The verb used is *enduesthai* and on it Burton writes: "The idiom conveyed no suggestion of putting on a mask, but referred to an act in which one entered into actual relations. . . . With a personal object it signifies 'to take on the character or standing' of the person referred to, 'to become'" (*op. cit.*, p. 204).

[18] See below, p. 114.

[19] Scott calls the argument about the baptism of the dead "obscure." It is not obscure, just uncomfortable. Schweitzer writes: "The baptism of the dead . . . is only explicable on the basis of the quasi-physical conception of the being-in-Christ. . . . It was only the consequence of his teaching about the being-in-Christ and his view of the effect of baptism that baptism for the dead could arise" (*Mysticism*, p. 286). Robinson too

Having been baptized into Christ, seized by God, and joined to the new creation, the individual is now under the control of the Holy Spirit, for it is the Holy Spirit who rules over that new creation. And it is the Holy Spirit who makes for us our confession of faith. Faith is a consequence of having been grafted into Christ, into that new realm where the Spirit rules. Our confession of faith is not really *our* confession at all, but the work of the Spirit active in us once we become part of the body of Christ. Again, Paul leaves no doubt as to the origin or source of faith. It is a consequence of baptism, the fruit of the Spirit. The key passage in this respect is probably I Cor. 12:3: "No one can say 'Jesus is Lord' except by the Holy Spirit." It is the Spirit who makes this confession for us. We are claimed by God, grafted into Christ, and in Christ we are under the Spirit and the Spirit works in us crying, "Abba, Father." That is precisely the order of events given in Gal. 4:6. First we are sons, that is, God claims us as his own. Then, because we are sons, the Spirit is in us. And it is the Spirit who cries out in us. Grammatically speaking, it is impossible to see this crying out as our work. It is the Spirit who cries out, making our confession of faith for us, for the participle *krazon* refers to the Spirit.[20]

This is the order of events: We are lost; we are seized by God and joined to Jesus; having been joined to Jesus, we are under the power of the Spirit. And the Spirit then makes our confession of faith for us. This is what Luther meant in his explanation of the Third Article of the Creed: "I believe that I cannot by my own reason or strength confess Jesus Christ as Savior and Lord except by the Holy Spirit."

The Holy Spirit's work, however, is not exhausted by simply making this confession of faith for us. Paul goes on to insist

---

acknowledges that the practice was a direct outgrowth of Paul's teaching concerning baptism (*op. cit.*, p. 54).

[20] See Burton's remarks, *op. cit.*, p. 221.

that every aspect of the Christian life, every virtuous and good thing manifested in our existence, is not our doing, but is the activity of the Spirit within us. Paul again is absolutely emphatic on this point, not allowing himself to be misunderstood; and it is precisely for this reason that he continually insists that there is no room for boasting in the Christian life. There is no room for boasting, not because boasting is a vice, but rather, there is nothing to boast about, for the Christian himself has done nothing (I Cor. 4:7)! Every virture of our life is the Spirit's doing. Notice, for example, Rom. 8:26. In that verse Paul clearly insists that we do not even know how to pray as we ought, but that here too the Spirit intercedes for us, making our prayers for us on our behalf, representing our unspoken yearnings before the Father. Or, to move into another direction, Paul (with Jesus) sums up the whole ethical activity of the Christian life in the single word "love." We are to love one another; love fulfills the whole law (Rom. 13:10; Gal. 5:14; Matt. 22:39-40). And yet it must be noted that the great love chapter of I Cor., ch. 13, is preceded by the last verse of I Cor., ch. 12, in which Paul flatly maintains that this love which fulfills the law is not an emotion of man created by man, but it is a gift of the Spirit — his doing. The same idea is seen in Rom. 5:5, where Paul stoutly maintains that "God's love has been poured into our hearts through the Holy Spirit which has been given to us."[21] Perhaps the most

[21] Barrett (*op. cit.,* p. 105) remarks that the genitive of Rom. 5:5 can be either subjective or objective and notes that many commentators (including Augustine) have taken it as objective. But Barrett prefers the subjective genitive. And in this he is correct — it is the Spirit who creates in us a recognition of the love that is God's. However, the Spirit also makes us able to love God, pouring into us not only an awareness of God's love toward us but our love toward him. It is even possible to take *tou theou* in an adjectival way, the Spirit being seen as bringing the Christlike or Godly love the Christian has to neighbor. In short, the very ambiguity of the phrase at this point is testimony to Paul's view of the comprehensiveness of the Spirit's activity.

exhaustive passage to this effect is in Gal. 5:22-23, where Paul sums up every single virtue of the Christian life and flatly insists that they are not the work of men but the fruit of the Spirit. He here insists that "love, joy, peace, patience, kindness, goodness," and faith (not "faithfulness," as the Revised Standard Version translates, but faith itself — the word used is *pistis*)[22] are all fruits of the Spirit. It must be noted how we return to basic themes. The theology of Paul is basically a simple and cohesive structure, and the same ideas return repeatedly. We insisted when discussing his conversion and his missionary activities above, that Paul sees man as open to the activity of supernatural forces outside him.[23] That idea recurs continually. Evil forces invade man ("It is . . . sin which dwells within me," Rom. 7:17). Good forces act in man ("It is Christ who lives in me," Gal. 2:20), and it is the Spirit who confesses our faith for us (I Cor. 12:3). Here the same idea of man open to the activity of external supernatural forces reappears with extraordinary force. Paul insists that every single virtue of the Christian life is a work of the Spirit. The Spirit is the energizing principle of the Christian life, and this is why the one constant imperative repeated in Paul's letters is the command not to quench the Spirit, not to grieve the Spirit — a phrase found at both ends of his letter-writing life (I Thess. 5:19; Eph. 4:30).

This stress upon man as open to the activity of supernatural forces we saw also to be confirmed in Paul's definition of man, for on statistical grounds we saw that Paul's language conveys the idea of man as helpless.[24] But at this point we come to an-

---

[22] And thus here too Paul stands squarely in the tradition of Jesus, for Jesus also had insisted that "faith," the confessing of the Father before men, was not a human effort but a divine activity of the Spirit — Luke 12:11-12: "Do not be anxious how or what you are to answer or what you are to say; for the Holy Spirit will teach you in that hour what you ought to say."

[23] See above, pp. 44-45.

[24] See above, p. 44.

The Body, Baptism, the Spirit

other key issue in Pauline theology. What does this enormous stress upon the Spirit as doing all, this stress upon God as the actor in baptism, do to the fact of human responsibility? We have already seen that the Satanward view of man as helpless is central to Pauline thought, but we also saw that, although it is central, it is not exclusive. There is also a strain in Pauline thought that insists upon man as free and responsible. How can these two opposing views be held together? The answer is found in Paul's doctrine of the Holy Spirit. In this doctrine, man's helplessness and man's responsibility merge together. Man is responsible — to do nothing! He is to submit to the Spirit who does all! Man's responsibility is negative — to be open to the Spirit, doing nothing of himself, but allowing the Spirit to do all.[25] This is an exceedingly difficult point to explain, and in attempting to do so, we shall use an illustration. The illustration is weak — too mechanical — and yet, if one reads sympathetically looking for the central idea involved, rather than searching out the weakness of the illustration itself, that central truth will emerge.

We can begin by saying that for Paul, man is lost. He is in a burning room, perishing. And, to make the illustration more dramatic, man is asleep in that burning room. He is being consumed and he does not even know it. That is what Paul means by being dead in one's trespasses (Eph. 2:1). Man cannot be more helpless than that — dead and unaware of it, asleep in a burning room and being consumed and unaware of it. At this point, however, a giant crane booms through the burning room. The Holy Spirit, that is, plunges into man's funeral pyre. This giant crane, the Spirit, reaches down into the flames and grabs the sleeping

---

[25] We take this to be Barth's view when he writes (*The Epistle to the Romans,* 6th ed., p. 110; London: Oxford University Press, 1933): "Nothing human which desires to be more than a void and a depression. . . . Only faith survives: faith which is not a work, not even a negative work; not an achievement, not even the achievement of humility; not a thing which exists before God and man in its own right."

man, wrenching him from the flames and carrying him toward safety. This is a work of God seeking us out — not a cooperative process of God and man in joint partnership, but a rescuing activity of "God alone" (as the Reformers would say), a rescuing activity dependent upon his will and his grace alone. The crane, having seized the man, has also awakened him. Aroused, awakened, man now sees the danger in which he once was and still is. The perilous trip is not over; it has just begun. And man, in his exposed position, in the grip of the crane, sees the flames leaping at him on all sides. Man is now awake — responsible. Man's responsibility is seen in that he has three avenues now open to him. He can reject the whole work of God, deliberately turning his back on the rescuing crane, spurning Word and Sacrament, and going back to the room from which he had earlier been extracted. In this case, if he turns back, salvation would be a work of God alone, as Luther said, but since he has cut himself off, damnation is now a work of man alone, again as Luther said. Or, to quote someone more recent than Luther, C. S. Lewis tells of two kinds of people: those who say to God, "Thy will be done," and those to whom God must reluctantly say, "Thy will be done." The latter have cut themselves off and are lost.

A second alternative is to recognize that God has begun a good work, and to endorse and embrace that good work. Man may endorse it and embrace it so enthusiastically that he decides to pitch in and help that work along. He starts to climb the superstructure of the crane. He turns to his own efforts as a supplement to God's activity. He starts to scramble up the crane. His motives are good, but in effect, what he is saying is that God's way is all right, but not quite good enough, not fast enough. He is declaring, unintentionally perhaps but nonetheless declaring, that God is insufficient and his actions inadequate and in need of supplementary human activity. This was the sin of the Galatians. The whole epistle to the Galatians makes it quite clear that it was not the intention of the Galatians deliberately to turn

The Body, Baptism, the Spirit

away from God, but rather, to anchor down and assure their status in Christ. Having been confused by the Judaizers, those who had begun in faith were trying to finish by works. They had turned to their own activity. The real antithesis of the epistle as Paul presents it is not one kind of human activity — works of the law — over against another kind of human activity — the response of faith; but rather, it is between human acts of any kind and a divine act. This must be God's work from beginning to end, not because God is jealous of his prerogatives, but rather, because any personal activity at all, whether man intends it to be so or not, is a declaration of independence from God. It is man's assertion that God's way is not good enough and that man, at least to some degree, cannot lean on God but must count on himself. Man's effort, no matter how well intentioned, is an accusation that God is insufficient.[26] That is, Paul is saying that even

---

[26] Rightly has Taylor noted that Luther has no doctrine of sanctification in his theology (*Forgiveness and Reconciliation*, p. 222). This is true because Luther was a profound student of Paul, and Paul has no doctrine of sanctification, no specific program of religious exercises to be followed (see Ch. 4, n. 15, above). This lack of a program of sanctification, a call to personal endeavor, is thus accounted for in a dual fashion. First, and positively, there is *no need* for man to do anything because the Spirit does all. Secondly and negatively, man *must not* do anything, for in trying to do so, he is rejecting God as insufficient. Even Bultmann recognizes the tragic fact that man can, despite his good intentions, end up rejecting God precisely because he manifests his zeal for God: "These words cannot mean 'I don't know how it happens that my good resolutions always get broken,' . . . for nothing is said about good resolutions that come to nothing in actual conduct. . . . Rather, the point of the passage in its context is that man brings about evil whereas according to his intention it was to be good. . . . In pursuing his 'desire' man thinks he is doing something good . . . and actually he is doing something evil. . . . The gruesome contradiction which characterizes human striving is being described" (*op. cit.*, p. 248). Again, Bultmann writes that sin is "both in the ignoring or transgressing of ethical demands and in excessive zeal to fulfill them. For the sphere of the flesh is by no means just the life of the passions, but is just as much that of the moral and religious efforts of man. . . . Whether then it is a matter of giving one's self up to worldly enticements and pleasures, either in frivolity or swept along by the storm

zeal itself — even such a thing as noble as zeal for the Lord — can be an evil and defiling thing. When man turns to his own efforts, no matter how lofty his goal, he has cut himself off from God, he has cried out: "God, you are not up to the task. Let me help you out!" Paul learned this the hard way, through experience. Before his conversion, he thought he was helping God by persecuting the church, trying to honor God by martyring the blasphemers. But after his conversion he came to see that he was not helping God but was fighting God. His noble early zeal was later seen to be not good, but evil, a foul and defiling thing. Zeal itself, a man's personal effort, no matter what the motive behind it, is vile. That is what Paul literally says in Phil. 3:8. Thinking back on his earlier acts of zeal for God, he calls them *skybalon,* literally refuse or excrement, human manure. Paul's Jewish background must be recalled. Those acts were not simply unnecessary, but they were positively evil, rendering him impure and defiled. Paul is insisting that any human act at all is really separation from God. Zeal itself is evil, and that is what he literally says in Gal. 5:20. One of the works of the flesh, one of the works of Satan active in the flesh, striving against the Spirit (the antithesis of the context, Spirit warring against Satan, is unmistakable), is zeal. The word is *zēlos,* zeal, not jealousy, as the Revised Standard Version mistakenly translates.[27] Man, then, if he starts to clamber up the crane, though his motives are good, is cutting himself off from God, telling God that he can go it alone. This is the

---

of passions or whether it is the zealous bustle of moral and religious activity that is involved — life in all these cases is an apostasy from God — a turning away from Him . . . to one's own strength, and is, therefore, enmity to God" (*Jesus and the Word,* pp. 239, 241; London: Ivor Nicholson and Watson, Ltd., 1935).

[27] Burton (*op. cit.,* p. 307) insists that "jealousy" is an interpretive assertion, not a translation. He insists that *zēlos* in classical Greek was always a noble passion, zeal as opposed to *phthonos* (envy). And this is the way Paul consistently uses the term — not as spiteful jealousy but as positive zeal, consecration to a noble purpose (Rom. 10:2; II Cor. 7:7, 11; 9:2; 11:2; Phil. 3:6).

The Body, Baptism, the Spirit

pathetic blindness of man. Even as he clambers toward God, he denies his goal. He struggles toward a God who is branded, by man's own struggles, as an insufficient God.

The third alternative is simply to hold still and do nothing. Submit to the Spirit. Quench not the Spirit. Grieve not the Spirit. Man's responsibility is focused in the fact that he is to do nothing and leave it to God. God will do in him and through him and for him all that must be done. Man is responsible — but responsible to hold still and not interfere with God's working, for salvation is of God alone. Paul emphatically cries out in Eph. 2:8, "For by grace you have been saved through faith." But no sooner has he said this than he recognizes that he has unintentionally left the door open. Faith might be misconstrued as a human act of the responsible individual. He has already said that faith is a work of God in the Spirit, but lest he be misunderstood, he emphatically states again, in the continuation of the sentence just quoted, "And this is not your own doing, it is the gift of God"!

God will do all. He will produce faith, our confession of faith, for us, produce our ethical life, give us gifts, place us in the ranks of service, achieve through us that which must be done. Man's sole responsibility is simply to submit to the Spirit. That is what accounts for the otherwise incomprehensible use of language that continually reappears in Paul. Note, for example, that in II Cor. 5:20 Paul writes, "We beseech you on behalf of Christ, be reconciled to God." An astounding bit of language! It is imperative, be reconciled, and yet it is a passive! Even in English the passive shows up, *be* reconciled! This is not something that man does, but something that is done on man and to which man submits.[28]

---

[28] On this verse, Taylor writes: " As we have already seen, although the verb 'be ye reconciled' is passive, it denotes an active process of cooperation on man's part. Man cannot accomplish his reconciliation with God, but he can refuse it" (*Forgiveness and Reconciliation*, p. 87). He is right in that man cannot accomplish this but can refuse it; but this does not mean that what is obviously a passive, and intended to be a passive, is to be made into an active. It is not cooperation that is demanded, but

Man's responsibility is simply to submit to the working of the Spirit without interfering. Precisely the same thing is found in Rom. 5:1, where the durative subjunctive is found. Paul does not say, as the Revised Standard Version translates, "We have peace with God," but he says, "Let us have peace with God." That is, his plea is to continue to submit to the Spirit, who has done this good work in you, who is pouring God's love into you (only four verses later).

The bulk of our discussion for this subject is now completed. It remains to draw several related conclusions out of the material already presented.

In the first place, one must be careful not to seek either to psychologize or to standardize the way in which God works. That is, there are some whom God reaches through baptism. Infant baptism has been with the church from the beginning. There are others whom God reaches through the preaching of the gospel, as adults, who are pricked in their consciousness before baptism. The two are not to be pitted one against the other as alternatives, but must be seen as complements, parts of a larger unity. This is why the Reformers spoke of the means of grace as both Word and Sacrament. God works through both, seizing men in baptism, and seizing men by the power of the proclaimed Word as well. That is why the Reformers, on one hand, insisted that the Word must be preached and on the other hand, insisted that the church was there only where the Sacraments were rightly administered. The whole thing is not to be grasped in a psychological sense, but must be seen in terms of theological orientation. The basic direction of *both* Word and Sacrament is downward. In both, God is the actor, seeking out man. This is not a cooperative process in which God reaches down to man in the Word, and man offers himself up in baptism. Nor is it man questing after God in faith. The direction of both

---

submission. It is precisely this cooperation, this personal zeal, which can rupture the relationship.

The Body, Baptism, the Spirit

Word and Sacrament is downward, for this is a theological picture of God in action.

A second observation: Notice how this crane illustration ties together the ancient rites of infant baptism and adolescent confirmation. In infant baptism, the crane seizes the child and claims him as God's own. But the child is unconscious, unaware of what took place. And then in the life of the church, he is instructed, told what took place, and at the age of responsibility, asked to confirm. To confirm what? To confirm that act of God which took place at baptism — asked to ratify or reject the uplifting hand of the Spirit. It is the baptismal covenant that is confirmed. Even as God had his own way at that moment, claiming us as his, so also now we vow that he will continue to have the leading of our life. In line with this, then, as long as we submit to the Spirit and bow to his leading, nothing can rip us out of the hand of that crane. Nothing in all of creation. This is the real key to Paul's doctrine of predestination. Predestination has nothing to do with an arbitrary or capricious selectivity on God's part, as if the crane seized some and rejected others. The doctrine is, instead, in Paul, exclusively a positive doctrine of comfort for the troubled believer. It is the assurance to the beleaguered saint, attacked from without and within by the hosts of Satan, that no evil force can separate us from God. It must be noted that Paul's specific references to predestination, in the Rom. 8:29 context and in the Rom., chs. 9 to 11, context, are sandwiched around one of the stirring shouts of victory of the New Testament (ch. 8:35 ff.). Predestination is not a story of God grabbing some and rejecting others. It is instead a positive doctrine that assures the attacked saint that as long as he submits to the Spirit, no other force will prevail against him.[29] It is because man is responsible

[29] Barrett recognizes this exclusively positive cast to Paul's doctrine of predestination: "Predestination is the most comfortable of all Christian doctrines, if men will accept it in its Biblical form, and not attempt to pry into it with questions which it does not set out to answer" (*op. cit.*, p. 171). The keen student sees a definite pattern emerging in theological

to submit to the Spirit, of course, that baptism for the dead is not a continuation of Pauline thought but a perversion of that thought. Baptism is not magical.[80] Man is responsible to submit to that which takes place. The dead could make no such responsible submission.

Finally, notice how the language of the crane affords the key to the otherwise impenetrable Pauline usage of language. We have already seen that salvation is a key term and is used primarily in the future tense.[81] But it is not used exclusively in the future. As even a cursory glance at a concordance reveals, Paul also uses the term occasionally in the present tense and even in the past tense. The crane grasped us in the past. We have been seized, we have been wrenched free, we have been saved — thus Eph. 2:5, 8 can use the perfect tense. We are even now being lifted up out of the burning room, we are being saved, in the present tense (I Cor. 1:18). But, finally and most significantly, at the return of Christ the saving action will be completed. Then the crane will have taken us out of the reach of the still-threatening flames. Then and then only will we be fully saved.

---

thought. C. H. Dodd rejects demonology and rejects the idea of man as enslaved by sin (Ch. 2, n. 3, above), and thus must conclude that predestination is the weakest point in Pauline theology (same note). Barrett, on the other hand, recognizes that Paul's thought is eschatologically orientated, and that salvation is primarily future (Ch. 5, n. 4, above). He also concedes that man is enslaved under Sin. On Rom. 7:17 he writes: "Sin is personified as an evil power which takes up its residence in human nature and there controls man's actions" (*op. cit.*, p. 147). Thus Barrett goes on to see predestination as comforting, the sounding of release for man from powers which he by himself could not resist.

[80] Schweitzer writes: "In Paul we have an unmediated and naked notion of sacrament such as is nowhere else to be met with" (*Paul and His Interpreters*, pp. 212–213). And yet he can go on to write elsewhere: "The effect of baptism and the Lord's Supper can be annulled by ungodly conduct" (*Mysticism*, p. 21). Robinson also writes: "There is, of course, nothing automatic about baptism. . . . Baptism places a man within the sphere where this grace is operative, but he may fall away with terrible consequences to his body, I Cor. 10:1 f." (*op. cit.*, p. 80).

[81] See Ch. 1, n. 6, above, and Ch. 5, n. 4, above.

CHAPTER 7

Christology, the Delay of the End

WE HAVE ALREADY SEEN that Paul keenly recognizes the true humanity of Jesus. He calls Jesus a "slave" of Satan and insists that Jesus has the same nature as we.[1] We have further seen that the Godward view, present in Paul, stresses the true humanity of Jesus — Jesus the true man, representing sinful humanity before God.[2] Paul continues to emphasize the true humanity of Jesus in such phrases as "fellow heirs with Christ" (Rom. 8:17), and in such contexts as I Cor. 15:28, where the subordination of Jesus to the Father is unmistakable.

But alongside the stress on the humanity of Jesus, there are very clear indications that Paul saw Jesus as more than man, as divine. The whole Satanward view, which we have seen to be primary in Paul, stresses Jesus as divine — "God was in Christ" — for only God is strong enough to stand up to so potent a foe. It is because Paul simply assumes the divinity of Jesus that he is able to write such a sentence as Rom. 9:5, which ends with the words "Christ, who is God over all, blessed forever." We will not dispute the fact that this is not the only possible interpretation. By a simple alteration of punctuation the phrase could end in an entirely different way, separating Christ from the adjectival

---

[1] See above, pp. 67–68; also Ch. 4, n. 14, above.
[2] See above, p. 67.

clause. In short, there is a real ambiguity here. But I would say two things to the ambiguity. (1) Paul, a strict Jew, never would have left himself open to misinterpretation that could ascribe divinity to Jesus unless he believed Jesus to be divine. In short, the very carelessness of language is on the side of those who would claim that Paul saw Jesus as divine. (2) There *is* an ambiguity. And that leads into the next point that must be made.

The fact that there is an ambiguity shows that Paul's Christology, at least at the time he wrote Romans, was not a carefully defined thing. He calls Jesus true man, and yet he calls Jesus' work the work of God, and he makes no clear Christological statements about Jesus that tie these two motifs together. He concentrates on the work of Christ as opposed to the person of Christ, and in those rare instances when he does make occasional or passing reference to the person of Jesus or his nature, those remarks are usually so vague and ambiguous that they are open to serious misinterpretation. For example, a wooden interpretation of Rom. 1:3-4 could lead to all sorts of difficulties. Verse 3, considered in isolation, could be taken as a complete repudiation of the virgin birth, and indeed has often been so taken. Or, v. 4 is open to an adoptionist Christology.[8] We hold neither one of these to be Paul's view, but to pursue the matter further here would be to take us from our major goal. The only point to be

---

[8] This is what justifies Barrett's remark: "Undoubtedly the earliest Christology had superficially an adoptionist tinge" (*op. cit.*, p. 20). Barth goes further (*op. cit.*, p. 30) and seeks to insist that it was only as a result of the resurrection that Jesus became the Son of God. However, the true point of Paul in the verse is not to dissolve the incarnation, but rather, to insist that in the resurrection, Jesus attained a level of superiority earlier denied him. The *en dunamei* is adjectival, modifying "Son of God," and not adverbial, modifying *horisthentos*. This is consistent with what we have said elsewhere, namely, that in the days of his flesh, Jesus was true God, and yet exposed to Satan. The resurrection did not alter whether he was God or not — it revealed his superiority to Satan, putting him beyond demonic attack.

Christology, the Delay of the End

made here is to insist that Paul, at least at this stage of his letter-writing life, had never bothered to develop a precise and carefully defined Christology. He is vague, ambiguous, and open to misinterpretation.

But later developments force him to develop a concise and explicit Christology in the Colossians and Ephesians epistles. To grasp fully the late developments that precipitated those epistles, we must first glance back over the life of Paul, seeing a continually recurring problem mounting in intensity, thrusting itself ever forward into the consciousness of Paul and the early church.

We begin by reminding ourselves of what we have seen to be the vital core of Pauline theology — the resurrection. "If there is no resurrection of the dead, . . . you are still in your sins. . . . Your faith is in vain. . . . We are of all men most to be pitied." Paul preached of Jesus as conquerer, Lord of all, triumphant over sin, death, and the devil.[4]

Now this emphasis caused the early Christians considerable difficulty. At Thessalonica, for example, Paul had been able to preach only three weeks before he was driven out of town by Jewish resistance (Acts 17:2, 5). Three weeks was only enough time to concentrate on the basic essentials of the Christian faith. And confined to essentials, Paul obviously stressed that which to him was so central — the victory of Jesus at the empty tomb that was to be culminated at the Parousia. Jesus the conquerer would return soon.

The Thessalonians learned this lesson well, indeed, almost too well. A careful reading of the two epistles makes it clear that they were so overwhelmed by the conviction of an imminent end that some had given up their jobs and were sitting waiting for the end to arrive. It is to caution them that there is no room for idleness in the Christian life — whether four minutes or four thousand years roll by, life is a tool to be used for Christ — that

[4] See above, pp. 76–77.

Paul writes to them, both pointing to his own industry as example and urging those who still work not to support the indolents (II Thess. 3:7 f.).

But although that was Paul's major concern in writing, it was not the major problem as far as the Thessalonians were concerned. What troubled them was the fact that between Paul's departure and his eventual arrival in Corinth some of the Thessalonian Christians had died. This was more than an emotional problem. It was a profound theological issue. For two reasons the Thessalonians had assumed that they were exempt from death. First, had not Paul been telling them that Christ was triumphant over death? Had he not assured them that Jesus was Lord, superior to the worst onslaughts of the devil? This Paul had said, and further, he had assured them that they belonged to Jesus. Thus it followed, they assumed, that they were exempt from death. Second, not only was Jesus superior but also his return was imminent. Thus, from this reasoning too, they expected not to die — because the end was near.

And yet some of their number had died. And this was the profound theological problem. Had those people been hypocrites? Was that why they died? Hardly a feasible answer, for perhaps they had lost their lives in the persecution that had followed their conversion and had driven Paul from town. They may have been martyrs for the faith. How could they be hypocrites? What then? Had they lost their reward in Christ because they had died? Was Jesus truly superior? Was he unable to protect those who were his? Were the dead in Christ lost? There is a dual problem here. One concerns the status of the dead in Christ. Have they forfeited anything or lost all? The other question, deeper, concerned the superiority of Jesus. Why was he unable to protect his own? It is an unasked but an implied question.

Paul ignores the implied question and answers only the immediate one. He assures the congregation that the dead in Christ

Christology, the Delay of the End 119

have lost nothing. That rather than having forfeited something, they have actually gained, for they will be the first to see Jesus as he returns in the imminent Parousia. That is the central point of the theological part of I Thessalonians, as a reading of I Thess. 4:13-18 makes clear.

But, to repeat, although Paul answers the problem concerning the dead in Christ, he ignores the deeper issues here. On the one hand, he does not treat the question of the superiority of Jesus. And on the other hand, he does not explain why death, having been conquered by Jesus, still continues in fact. Maybe Paul ignores these questions (or to be more exact, he does not ignore them, but instead, explicitly rejects them, cf. I Thess. 5:1) because the Thessalonians are too new in the faith to wrestle with such issues, having been evangelized for only three weeks. Or maybe Paul does not yet have such answers even for himself. In any event, because he does not answer these questions about the superiority of Jesus and how it can be that death, conquered, still continues, these questions continue to thrust themselves on Paul. We have seen how he does eventually come to explain how it can be that death is beaten in principle but continues in fact. In I Cor., ch. 15, he tells us that each in his own order, first Christ, and then at his coming those who belong to Christ, shall be freed of death. A war is going on, the war still continues, but the crucial battle is in the past. Thus we can rejoice even in the midst of war. Knowing that if we fall, our leader will rescue us, the enemy is thus deprived of eternal significance.[5]

But one answer produces another problem. Having explained the relationship between resurrection and Parousia, having made it clear that the continuing interval was in no way to be seen as a contradiction to Christ's Lordship, having made it clear that Jesus was truly superior and would fully destroy the enemy in the future, Paul found another problem thrusting itself forward.

[5] See above, pp. 90–91.

Since Christ is stronger, and since, therefore, the time of the end is totally under his control, why is there a delay? If what Paul says is true about the superiority of God in Christ, why, then, does he tarry and allow his troops to fall in battle? What is the purpose of this delay? Is it an evidence of lack of compassion in God? Is he indifferent to the suffering of the elect, allowing them to be continually exposed to the counterattack of Satan? Or is it an evidence of the lack of power of God? The fact of the failure of the Parousia to materialize caused old problems to return with renewed intensity. What was God waiting for? Or maybe he was not waiting at all. Maybe the delay was not optional on his part. Maybe he had not chosen to wait, but was instead being forced to wait. That is, perhaps the original claim of the superiority of Christ was not valid. Perhaps the enemy was sufficiently strong to rebuff the advance of God's Kingdom.

It was true, as anyone with an open mind could see, that at a given time in the past Jesus was truly stronger. The empty tomb was evidence enough of that fact. But it was also true that at least at one time in the past the enemy had been strong enough to prevail. Paul himself had said this, in I Cor. 2:8, where he flatly insists that the crucifixion of Jesus was the work of the rulers of this age, the spiritual host of wickedness in the heavenly places. If they had been able to prevail once in the past, perhaps they were able to prevail once more. True, they had been beaten at the resurrection, but perhaps their recuperative powers had allowed them to regroup themselves and they were now, if not superior to Jesus, at least equal to him, and this is why the end failed to come. These evil hosts of wickedness, the celestial powers and principalities, were fighting a successful delaying action. The failure of the end to come was due, not to a decision of God, but to the resistance of the foe.

There was much factual material that could be summoned to support such a hypothesis. It just simply could not be denied

Christology, the Delay of the End   121

that the enemy seemed to be waxing steadily stronger ever since the resurrection. The story of the postresurrection period, it is true, is a story of the advance of the gospel from humble surroundings to the heart of the Empire, Rome itself. But coupled with this advance was a corresponding counteradvance, equally real for those who were living through that period. That is, for every great forward wave of God's purpose, there was a counterforce rolling back and nullifying Christian gains. And the gains that were made were achieved at a frightful cost of human suffering. Paul lists some of the agonies that he had undergone for the propagation of the gospel.[6] But what must be noted further is the progressive increasing, rather than decreasing, of those sufferings. The farther Paul went, the greater the problems. At first, it was only the resistance of the Jews. They opposed him because he was implying that they, not believing in Jesus, were not true Jews. He was disinheriting them, and they attacked him.[7] And later, it was the non-Christian Gentiles who attacked Paul. The officials, the administrators, those charged with the maintenance of order, beat him and jailed him, often without a fair hearing. And the circle of enemies spread. In Galatia, not only non-Christian Jews but also Christian Jews, Judaizers, opposed him and attacked him, undermining his work and accusing him of presenting a mutilated and truncated gospel, denying his apostleship, and hypnotizing his converts. And then, in Corinth, not only non-Christian Gentiles but also Gentile converts opposed him. His own congregation turned on him and accused him of impotence and two-facedness, insisting that he was a

---

[6] See above, pp. 84–85.

[7] The same line of reasoning that had earlier offended Paul (see above, p. 36) was now offending those Jews to whom Paul preached. This fact, coupled with the further fact that his preaching appealed to the proselytes and succeeded in winning over large numbers of the converts they had made in many years of labor, were probably the two basic reasons for their hostility to Paul, and to Christian missionaries in general.

weak and colorless man, rejecting his leadership. The enemies of Paul had come to include every color of the human spectrum, ranging all the way from non-Christian Gentiles and Jews to Christian Gentiles and Jews. Paul saw the hand of Satan behind those activities of opposition, and he called his enemies servants of the devil (II Cor. 11:13-15).

In short, the enemy, rather than fading away, seemed to be waxing stronger, his opposition increasing. Instead of acting like a beaten foe with a shattered spinal column, the enemy grew in power, not only becoming stronger but apparently prevailing. The basic goal of Satan seemed to be to hinder Paul from visiting his people (I Thess. 2:18). And now Satan seemed to be succeeding. For at the time of Colossians-Ephesians, Paul was in jail. He was muzzled, unable to preach the gospel, his voice stilled. Earlier, he had, it is true, faced opposition, but at least he was free to travel and preach. Now even that was denied him. Two long years in Palestinian prisons were succeeded by two years of house arrest in Rome. And even more than imprisonment, Paul knew that martyrdom was a very real possibility. He knew that he might soon be poured forth as a libation, an offering of faith (Phil. 2:17). In the Roman prison, his ear was to the wall and he could hear the rumblings coming from the palace of the Caesars. Already there had been one expulsion of Jews from Rome under Claudius (Acts 18:2), and the Roman were becoming increasingly perceptive with the passing of years. They were coming to recognize that it was not the Jews in general who were causing trouble, but it was instead the fact that the Jews were reacting to and rejecting the message of Christ that was causing all the difficulty. When the Christians came in, rioting followed. And therefore the suspicion of Rome was narrowing down to the Christians. The centuries of persecution were about to begin. Paul knew that his own impending death was not to be unique. It threatened to become the universal experience of the church. The enemy seemed to be waxing stronger.

Not only was he in prison, unable to continue working into the future, but at the same time, his work of the past was crumbling around his ears. He had spent his adult life founding churches for Jesus Christ, and that work cannot now be sentimentalized and glorified. By every standard of human evaluation, Paul seemed to be a failure. In Galatia, where he had purchased converts literally at the cost of his own blood, those converts seemed to be deserting the cross of Jesus Christ. Paul had cried out in anguish: "O foolish Galatians! Who has bewitched you, before whose eyes Jesus Christ was publicly portrayed as crucified? . . . I am afraid I have labored over you in vain" (Gal. 3:1; 4:11).[8] The work failed, the church disappeared in Asia Minor. At Thessalonica too, another place where his work was carried out only at the cost of great personal suffering, his congregation seemed indifferent to the responsibilities of the Christian, and he had to scold them for their laziness by advising that he who did not work should not eat (II Thess. 3:6-13). Even at Corinth, apparently one of his most successful congregations, where he had worked for eighteen months, his converts were not only spurning him but were apparently indifferent to the most elementary precepts of the gospel. And thus Paul had to cry out that there were evidences of immorality to be found which were absent in even the crassest pagan setting — there was a man sleeping with his own mother (I Cor. 5:1).

This is what Paul sees after a lifetime of labor. All seems to be decaying, crumbling away. His voice is stilled, his death is a real possibility, and his work is eroding. The enemy is waxing even stronger. Paul himself recognizes this growth of enemy

[8] The verb *baskainō* in Gal. 3:1 means to bewitch, in the sense of to overpower, to sweep one off one's feet. It has a nuance of magic, the idea of the evil eye (Burton, *op. cit.,* p. 144). This is consistent with Paul's view of man, which sees man as exposed to malignant supernatural forces able to possess a man.

power and this is why the note of demonology in Paul's closing epistles is painted in far deeper hues, more ominous tones, than anywhere else in his earlier life. It is in Ephesians, one of his last epistles, that the awesome picture of the frightful power of the enemy is fully presented (Eph. 6:12).

But it is not only Paul who sees this growth of enemy resistance. His converts see it also. They are thinking people who cannot faith to see the frightful capacity for evil of the supposedly beaten foe. Therefore, because of the failure of the end to come and the growth of enemy opposition, the congregation at Colossae is beginning to doubt the sufficiency of Jesus, beginning to doubt the true Lordship and superiority of Jesus. The old problem of the Thessalonians returns with a vengeance. The Colossians, because of this doubt, are apparently beginning to believe that the work of Jesus is incomplete and that they must turn to supplementary activities of their own to finish up his work. In short, it appears that they feel that Jesus went only just so far in his work, and now they must turn to their own efforts to complete that work. The Colossians are not apostates, rejecting Christ; they are, on the contrary, consecrated people trying to protect and preserve and anchor down their status in Christ. The problem at Colossae is very similar to that at Galatia earlier, but it springs from a different source. At Galatia the congregation had been led to doubt the sufficiency of Jesus' work because of the words of the Judaizers. That is, they had come to look upon the gospel as truncated and abridged. The Judaizers had maintained that Paul had given them only part of the truth. Faith in Jesus was demanded, even as Paul had said, but Paul had not said enough. In addition to faith, there was to be personal activity in accordance with the law. And thus the Galatians, having begun in faith, were turning to supplemental actions of their own, finishing in works. The Colossians found themselves in similar straits for different reasons. They too had begun in faith and

Christology, the Delay of the End

were now turning to supplemental actions of their own, the observance of dietary rules and pagan religious rituals (Col. 2:16 ff.). The only difference was that their actions were prompted, not by the interference of outsiders come into their midst, but by their own experiences and observations. The failure of the end to come and the apparent growth of enemy power convinced them that something supplemental was needed. It was for this reason that the Colossians (whom Paul calls "saints and faithful brethren," ch. 1:2) were actually on the verge of worshiping the angel powers (ch. 2:18), no doubt in an attempt to appease them and thus ward off those evil powers who had not yet been subjugated fully by the activities of Jesus.

To this problem Paul addresses himself. In the first place, Paul argues, as he did at Galatia, that these supplemental practices are not only not necessary, but they are downright dangerous. Even though the Galatians had noble motives — to bulwark and protect and supplement their status in Christ — their actions were in reality not benefiting their situation, but jeopardizing it. By taking up the law they were in reality severing themselves from Christ, crying out that what God could not do, they would do for themselves, hence declaring God insufficient unto the needs of men.[9] Their actions were in reality a return to a yoke of bondage. (Gal. 5:1.) They were returning to the slavery under the elemental spirits of the cosmos (ch. 4:9), for they were identifying themselves not only with the law, which had fallen under demonic powers, but with those demonic powers themselves. Paul develops exactly the same arguments here in Colossians. He argues that no matter how well intentioned the Colossians may be, in reality their ascetic practices and self-abasement is not placating the desires of the flesh and the powers of evil, but instead, those actions are, on the contrary, inflaming the flesh and worsening their status. That is the true rendering of Col. 2:23,

[9] See above, pp. 108–109.

where he insists that those actions are "of no value, serving only to indulge the flesh."[10] By turning to their own efforts, they are simultaneously rejecting the work of God and affirming their own powers, insisting that what Jesus could not do, they can do. They "indulge" the flesh and excite their own mistaken ideas of independence. It is not without its own significance that it is at this very time of his life, in prison in Rome, that Paul also writes Philippians, where he recalls that his own efforts, a turning to his own zeal, was a defiling thing, excrement, defiling him rather than helping him.[11] And it is also at this time that he writes the parallel epistle, Ephesians, insisting as forcefully as he can (ch. 2:8) that salvation is a work of God and of God alone.[12]

Now, thus far, Paul's argument has been in one sense negative. He tells them that they are not to turn to their own efforts because in reality this is a rejection of Christ. Paul goes on to be positive, telling them also why such supplementary activity is not necessary. Despite all their doubts, despite the waxing stronger

---

[10] The phrase of Col. 2:23, *ouk en timēi tini pros plēsmonēn tēs sarkos,* is admittedly a very difficult one. The problem centers in the word *plēsmonē,* which is used nowhere else in the New Testament. The word means repletion, satiety, satisfaction, or gratification. Thus a literal rendering would say, "These things are of no value for the satisfaction of the flesh." From this ambiguous statement two alternatives emerge: (1) "these things are of no value in checking the indulgence of the flesh" and (2) "these things are of no value, serving only to indulge the flesh." Arndt and Gingrich state that the Greek exegetes took the phrase in the former sense, insisting that these things were valueless; but they go on to insist that in view of the way *sarx* is used in v. 18 the word is "surely to be taken in a bad sense," meaning that these things are not irrelevant or valueless; but rather, they constitute a positive danger, indulging and arousing the desires of the flesh. This is the view taken also by Knox (*St. Paul and the Church of the Gentiles,* p. 171), who writes in a paraphrase of the verse that these things which have an appearance of value are not means for destroying the influence of the body over the soul, but a "positive means of gratifying the flesh and increasing its influence."

[11] See above, p. 110.
[12] See above, p. 111.

Christology, the Delay of the End

of the enemy, Christ is not insufficient and inferior. It is at this point that Paul develops his Christology in great detail, insisting eloquently and ardently that Jesus truly is superior because he is both Creator and Conqueror of those evil God-opposing forces.

Let us look at these two affirmations: Christ as Creator and as Conqueror. First, Christ is the creator and controller of these evil forces. They may be powerful, but whatever power they have, they are, nonetheless, not independent. They are creatures subordinate to Jesus, for it is he who called them into being. Whatever else is said about the dualism of the New Testament, this must be said — it is a limited dualism, not of the Manichaean type. There are not two coequal and coeternal forces forever opposed to each other, neither of which is able to prevail. The dualism of the moment is real. Satan is truly opposed, not a servant in disguise. Yet those forces were once good, in the past, and will be conquered, in the future. The creator aspect of Christ deals with the past. The conqueror aspect of Christ deals with the future. The evil forces are creatures subordinate to Jesus, for he created them. That is the essential thrust of the whole first chapter of Colossians. From ch. 1:15 onward we read: " He is the image of the invisible God, the first-born of all creation; for in him all things were created, *in heaven* and on earth, visible *and invisible,* whether thrones or dominions or principalities — [all exceedingly significant titles in the light of the parallel in Eph. 6:12, where these principalities are by definition the archenemies of God] *all things* were created through him and for him. He is before all things, and in him all things hold together." [13]

---

[13] The usual approach to these verses is to maintain that here Paul is arguing against and adopting the language of Gnosticism. This is not so. Gnosticism was not a competitor of primitive Christianity but a consequence of primitive Christianity. There is no solid scientific evidence that Gnosticism was, in the first century, a cohesive verbalized system of specu-

Christ, then, is Creator. But Paul goes on. When those created beings went berserk and ran amuck, when the fall of the angels took place as apocalyptic writing recounts it, God in Christ once more reasserted his superiority by conquering those evil forces. It is at this point that we can return to Col. 2:14-15. We have already noted that Paul, in these verses, actually dares to reverse the imagery of the cross, showing Jesus as the aggressive one,

---

lation. There are points of contact that exist between first-century cosmological thought and later Gnostic structures, but they are only points and not lines of development. But commentators, having rejected demonology as a formative factor in Paul's thought, are obliged to search elsewhere, therefore, for the source of Paul's logic, and they claim to find that source in Gnosticism, even if it means dragging Gnosticism forward a full century to satisfy their claims. Hence, we find scholars simultaneously affirming that Gnosticism as a system is late, and yet it must be early! Howard C. Kee and Franklin W. Young are typical of this approach. They begin by dating Gnosticism in the second century: "By the second century of the Christian era, gnosticism had developed into elaborate systems of theology and cosmic speculation" (*Understanding the New Testament,* p. 20; Prentice-Hall, Inc., 1957). And then they proceed in the very next sentence to drag it forward one full century and more: "But the basic elements were present long before the beginning of Christianity." To repeat, this attempt to date Gnosticism earlier than the evidence allows is due to the fact that no other source can be found for Paul's arguments in Colossians. However, if one accepts seriously the precepts of demonology, Paul's development flows naturally from those sources and no outside interfering factor need be found. A strong case can be made for maintaining that the Gnosticism of the second century is a direct product or consequence of — not competitor of — Pauline thought. After Paul, when the end still failed to materialize, two lines of thought were open. On the one hand, one could say that Jesus did not return because there was *no need* for him to return. Or one could say that Jesus did not return because he was *unable* to return. That is, demonology could either grow stronger or else disappear. One could say that the world was already under the hand of God, and it was not necessary for Jesus to return and cleanse the cosmos. Or one could say that the world was so firmly gripped by evil forces that God would not be able to cleanse the world and that the only escape, therefore, was to get out of the fallen world. The limited dualism of the New Testament could either disappear or develop into radical or absolute dualism. Both of these routes were followed. The theology of Hebrews

Christology, the Delay of the End

doing the nailing, standing hammer in hand.[14] This is not a sudden impulse or a flare for the dramatic. This imagery is demanded by the circumstances. We have just seen that in I Cor. 2:8, Paul said that the evil powers had crucified Jesus, and then Paul went on to insist in I Cor., ch. 15, that in the resurrection Jesus had conquered them. The resurrection posed no problem. It was the crucifixion that troubled the Colossians. If the evil forces were able in the past to prevail, at the cross, perhaps they were once more that powerful and able to prevail again. Thus it is that the crucifixion itself, and not simply the triumph over death, is that which must be stressed and reinterpreted. Paul thus argues that it is not true that they prevailed at the cross. Even there, in that event of Golgotha, it was Christ Jesus who was in charge. It was he who was in command, subduing the

---

dismisses demonology, setting it aside — the ministering spirits of Heb., ch. 1, are good, servants of God. Suffering in Heb., ch. 12, is no longer seen as an attack of Satan but as a judgment of God. God is in control. Hence, eschatology also can wane, for the hope for the end of the world was based upon the prior assumption that something was wrong with the world. And that is what happens in Hebrews. Eschatology comes to be seen in other than Pauline-Synoptic terms and develops instead along Platonic lines — two kingdoms not succeeding each other, but running simultaneously in time, right now with those unseen realities. This is the way the early church eventually adjusted itself to the failure of the Parousia to materialize. If C. H. Dodd would make a case for "realized eschatology," he ought not to turn to Paul and the Synoptics but to Hebrews, and, to a lesser extent, to John. But Gnosticism took the other fork. It developed a radical dualism, insisting that Jesus did not return because this world was forever under evil powers. In both cases eschatology disappeared, a hope for an end of this evil cosmos evaporated, one side concluding that the world was not evil and this was why Jesus did not return, and the other side concluding that the evil forces were too strong to allow Jesus to return. In both instances, though the conclusions go off in different directions, the conclusions were precipitated by the disappointment of the primitive Christian eschatological expectation. This is an enormous subject and will have to be dealt with in greater depth in a separate work, for to pursue it here would lead us too far afield.

[14] See above, p. 77.

rebels, manifesting his superiority, showing himself as conqueror, standing hammer in hand doing the nailing.

Paul has now sketched out his Christology — Jesus the Creator, Jesus the Conqueror. It is not a Greek Christology, concentrating on the person of Jesus per se, but a Hebrew Christology, stressing the acts of Jesus, showing Jesus as doubly stronger than the foe that seems so strong. Yet one more problem remains. If all this is true, as Paul has argued, why then does that enemy, so inferior to Jesus, still continue? How can the delay of the Parousia and the continuing activity of the enemy be explained? This, after all, was the problem from the beginning, for it seemed to be an accusation of God's weakness, his inability to return and finish off the foe.

Paul, in a fashion typical of him, reverses the situation and turns an accusation into an affirmation, showing how the delay is not an evidence of God's weakness, but instead, a manifestation of his purpose. Something is supposed to be happening in this continuing moment between resurrection and return. God could, if he would, destroy the enemy immediately, ending all resistance and liberating the church. But if he did, the enemy would be cut down right in the middle of their diabolical resistance and thus would be eternally lost. Paul argues that God does not wish this. The seeking, redemptive love of God that reaches for us reaches for them also. They too are God's creatures, objects of his love. And therefore, God is delaying in order to give them an opportunity to hear the word of reconciliation and come to the knowledge of the truth.[15] This motif, God seeking to bring

---

[15] I noted earlier, p. 59, that Paul uses the words concerning "reconciliation" only a limited number of times, and that a surprisingly large percentage of that limited number of usages is found in Colossians-Ephesians. The reason for that ought to be clear now, in that Paul uses these words in respect to the cosmic host of evil heavenly figures. *They* can be reconciled — *for them* the word makes sense, for they are not enslaved, as is man, but they are rebellious.

Christology, the Delay of the End

back even the rebellious heavenly host, is a dominant idea of these closing epistles of Paul's life: Colossians, Ephesians, and Philippians. For example, Phil. 2:10 carefully insists that the redemptive work of Jesus extends not only to man, but Paul instead literally insists that at the name of Jesus *every* knee should bow, not just the human ones on earth, but also those above and below the earth — a powerfully meaningful phrase in the light of Eph. 6:12, where he defines those above the earth as the prime enemies of God.

The same concept is seen in Col. 1:20. Here again, Paul flatly says that the purpose of God is that through Christ *all* things might be reconciled to God. The language is unmistakable. And again, in Eph. 3:10, Paul once more insists that the plan of God is now being made known to the principalities and powers in the heavenly places, and at the risk of being overly repetitious, we must remind ourselves anew that it is in this very epistle, only three chapters later, that Paul identifies these powers and principalities as the spiritual host of wickedness in the heavenly places, the world rulers of this present darkness, the basic enemies of God.[16]

This, then, is Paul's final answer as to why the end has not come immediately and why the enemies are tolerated. They could be destroyed at once, but then they would be lost. God in his infinite love is reaching for his creatures. Paul has taken an accusation of God's impotence and made it an affirmation of God's love. The Christian concedes that this is right, and thus,

[16] Note how Paul's maturing views have reversed the view of the early church. At the outset, the early church entered into no missionary activity, believing that angels would gather the elect (see above, pp. 47–48). But now Paul is insisting that it is men who will gather the angel powers, "that through the church the manifold wisdom of God might now be made known to the principalities and powers in the heavenly places" (Eph. 3:10). The church is the body of Christ, the ongoing incarnate Jesus, and by definition, higher than the angels. Hence, the logic of Paul in such places as I Cor. 6:3, "Do you not know that we are to judge angels?"

just like Jesus in the days of his flesh, the Christian is attacked by the enemy forces, and in some measure his suffering parallels that of Jesus. In love, he endures the attacks of the enemy (Col. 1:24).

In conclusion, several remarks must be made. It is granted, with no argument whatever, that this is an exceedingly difficult argument. It is not difficult to comprehend, for the words and logic are quite clear. But they are difficult to apply. It is difficult to speak of evil spiritual powers in a scientific age that refuses to take these things seriously. How much more difficult, then, to maintain that the very reason for the delay is that these celestial foes might be converted. I would insist, nonetheless, that even if one is not willing to accept obvious Pauline intent, there is still enormous significance for the church in these words. In the first place, notice that Paul is defining the significance of history. He is making the staggering claim that the only reason that the world continues on at all is that the work of God in Christ might be extended to all creatures. He is making the fantastically exciting assertion that the only reason life continues in this world is so that the church might be about its business. And in this claim he is defining not only history but also the church. The fundamental task of the church is not to create architectural marvels to edify city street corners, nor is its purpose to provide recreational centers where children can play beanbag, but the fundamental purpose of the church — its only *raison d'être* — is to preach the gospel! Rightly did the Reformers insist that the Word must be preached!

Notice also the image of God that grows out of Paul's logic. If the unfathomable love of God reaches even for the evil heavenly host, if he loves even them, then there is hope for you and me.

CHAPTER 8

A Study in Demythologizing

I HAVE TALKED MUCH, directly and indirectly, about demonology and eschatology. This has been the hub out of which Pauline theology has grown. The dogmas of Paul are spokes that grow out of this central hub. His concept of the church, of the nature of man, and of the resurrection were determined by the assumption of the validity of demonology-eschatology. It follows, therefore, that anyone who rejects these twin motifs as the central hub will also have to reject the dogmas pertaining to man, to Christ, to the resurrection, etc., which grow out of that hub. Theology is an essentially simple thing. Secondary ideas grow out of primary concepts, and thus when primary concepts are rejected, there is a transformation of thought across the entire sweep of theological structure. In my estimation, the tragedy of contemporary theology is that theology has failed to accept the hub of demonology-eschatology. As a result, much of contemporary Christianity has been deformed. This process of rejecting demonology-eschatology is called *demythologizing,* that is, getting rid of the myth, the archaic, no longer valid world view. And this process has resulted in compromise, distortion, and downright perversion of basic Christian concepts about the nature of man, the nature of sin, the significance of the resurrection, and the role of the Spirit. It has created a drastically new orientation of all the spokes we mentioned earlier.

The leader of the whole movement is Rudolf Bultmann. Although I would admit that Bultmann is perhaps the greatest New Testament theologian of our day, I would nonetheless insist that he has been given far more credit than he deserves. What I mean is that Bultmann did not produce a movement called demythologizing, but rather, that movement produced Bultmann. He did not set off a process that did not exist earlier, but instead, he articulated and verbalized a process that antedated him, and on that articulation he rode to fame. He became a spokesman for an already existent movement. He was not Saint George who slew the ancient dragon of old. He did not kill Satan — he was merely a pallbearer at the funeral. Satan had been killed or ignored or neglected by theologians for several theological generations before Bultmann ever took the field.[1] Bultmann does not

---

[1] We have already noted the way in which James Denney rids his thought of demonology; he just simply ignores the "mythological" figure of Satan (see Ch. 2, n. 2, above). This is the same method used, more recently, by Vincent Taylor. In his many volumes on the New Testament, there is no sustained treatment of Satan to be found anywhere. Another method of demythologizing is that of C. H. Dodd. In effect, he is insisting that there is no need to demythologize because the New Testament never intended to be taken literally in respect to either demonology or eschatology. That is, he denies these twin motifs any legitimacy. One of the continuing theses of his book *The Parables of the Kingdom* is that the future tenses of Jesus were simply an accommodation of language, poetical imagery, symbolic terminology, and the eschatological hope of the church was due to the church's failure to recognize the nonliteral cast to Jesus' speaking (see especially *Parables,* p. 108). In the same way, Dodd denies any metaphysical content to Paul's language, reducing that also to poetical imagery (see Ch. 2, n. 3, above). Edward Langton, whom we have already seen finding fault with Denney's ignoring of Satan (Ch. 2, n. 2, above), also finds fault with a method, such as Dodd's, that would deny demonology, reducing Jesus' remarks to an accommodation of language. In *Essentials of Demonology* (London: The Epworth Press, 1949), pp. 222–223, he writes: "Never for a moment does He [Jesus] seem to doubt that demons exist and that they afflict the lives of men as they were popularly believed to do. . . . Theories of accommodation do not accord well with the character of Jesus as the teacher of divine truth. They leave us with

A Study in Demythologizing

represent something new. He is not qualitatively different from other theologians active today; he is only quantitatively different. He goes farther than most in his demythologizing, and this is why one sees in his work, more clearly than in that of others, the eventual end results of setting aside Satan. If there is any qualitative difference between Bultmann and others, it is that he does consciously and aggressively and thoroughly what was earlier done naïvely or unreflectingly or inconsistently.

We can look upon Bultmann, then, as typical of a process of rejection of Satan in contemporary theology, and in examining a few key factors in his thought, one can see clearly what was meant above when I said that if we reject the hub of Paul's thought, we reject the spokes as well.

We begin by noting this — that Bultmann, without argument,

---

the problem of explaining why He should deliberately have strengthened about the minds of His disciples the bonds of a false theory which have never been relaxed, at least until the modern period." In another work, *Satan, A Portrait,* p. 114, he enters into another extended rejection of theories of accommodation, summoning as support an extended quotation from Bishop Gore. But, despite his denunciation of Denney and his rejection of theories such as Dodd's, Langton, in the final analysis, ends up in exactly the same position as his foes. The only difference is that they reject Satan or ignore Satan without examining the evidence, and he rejects demonology after examining the evidence. Langton concludes: "If therefore we are compelled to hold that Jesus believed in, and frequently affirmed, the existence of Satan and the demons, the further question remains: Does His teaching in this respect correspond to reality? In other words, Does Satan exist as the head of the kingdom of evil which embraces a vast host of evil spirits who continually seek to injure and destroy men? The conclusion we have arrived at is that we are not compelled to accept this teaching as ultimate reality merely because it formed a part of the teaching of Jesus. For, as we have seen, in His incarnate condition Jesus was avowedly limited in knowledge" (*Essentials,* p. 223). Bultmann is not an innovator or pioneer. Theologians have for a long time been rejecting demonology. The ways in which it is done — one ignores, one denies, one dismisses it as a product of Jesus' human limitations — are, like the demons themselves, legion in number. At least in this sense New Testament theologians are Biblical — they are casting out demons.

agrees that the basic hub of Jesus' thought is demonology-eschatology.[2] Bultmann has one of the most penetrating statements in all of modern theology about the centrality of demonology in the thought of Jesus. On practically the first page of his great two-volume work on the theology of the New Testament, Bultmann writes: "Jesus' message is connected with the hope . . . which is primarily documented by the apocalyptic literature, a hope which awaits salvation not from a miraculous change in historical (i.e., political and social) conditions, but from a cosmic catastrophe which will do away with the conditions of the present world as it is. The presupposition of this hope is the pessimistic-dualistic view of the Satanic corruption of the total world complex."[3] To repeat, this is one of the most powerful affirmations of the centrality of demonology in all of contemporary theology. The lifetime studies of this fine scholar have convinced him that the thought of Jesus grows directly out of apocalyptic and that that thought is based upon the conviction that the entire world is under Satanic domination. Therefore, Jesus looked for the end of this world. The demonology, the conviction that this world was evil, produced the eschatology, the hope for a new cleansed cosmos.

But although that view was central for Jesus, Bultmann says, in effect: "Let us be honest before God and man.[4] Let us openly

---

[2] Here Bultmann has made a real contribution. There is something basically dishonest, or, if that is too harsh, at least something fundamentally unscholarly in the frantic attempts of the past to rid theological thought of demonology, pretending that it is not there, or rejecting the obvious intent of words, or dismissing it as the product of Jesus' ignorance. Bultmann puts an end to the word games, and demands that we recognize that even though these motifs may not make sense to us in our day, they were basic to Jesus and the early church in their day.

[3] *Theology of the New Testament*, Vol. I, pp. 3–4. See also his affirmation of demonology in Paul's epistles, Ch. 5, n. 1, above.

[4] This is an allusion, of course, to Robinson's recent book *Honest to God*, which is Bultmann rewritten for the layman.

A Study in Demythologizing

avow the fact that although this was basic to Jesus, it is irrelevant and nonvalid in our time." This is the thesis of Bultmann — that by concentrating on these motifs, valid to Jesus but not valid to the modern man, the church enters into the danger of obscurantism. Even though Jesus accepted these facts, not even the most Bible-pounding fundamentalist today truly accepts them, no matter what he may say on the surface. The basic belief that Satan is active in this world, producing suffering and tragedy, is flatly maintained without qualification by Jesus in Luke 13:16. Jesus stands before the crippled woman and in language not to be misinterpreted — in clear and unambiguous terms — he insists that for eighteen years *Satan* has bound this woman. But whether Jesus says it or not, no one today believes it! Even the most pious of us just do not accept that fact! The proof is in our actions. Where do we go when we have a headache? To the pharmacist for aspirin or to the pastor for prayer? The answer is obvious, and the implication is enormous. By the very fact that we go to aspirin and not the altar we are insisting in fact that, no matter what we say in theory, pain is not a theological problem, that sickness is a medical, not a clerical, consideration. More extreme examples can be given. When a loved one gets cancer, it is true that we turn to prayer, but nonetheless, we turn to the finest surgeon we can procure and we support the cancer fund solicitations, and these actions testify to our basic conviction that this is not a theological issue but a medical one, and that man, given enough time, will overcome the dilemma, not through piety, but through research and improved operating techniques. This is the viewpoint of modern man, and Bultmann is right — there is no debate — when he tells us that this *is* modern man's view, both in the church and without.

Or take the other example, eschatology. It is true that every time we open our mouths to say the Apostles' Creed we are giving shape to our eschatological hope for a real end to the world — "from thence he shall come to judge the quick and the dead . . . the resurrection of the body." But, do we really, honestly, and unwaveringly believe what we are saying? How many of us, when we wake up in the morning, are surprised that we woke up in the morning and that the world did not end? How many of us, as we walk the streets in the daytime, have our eyes fastened on the heavens, literally waiting for Jesus to break through the clouds surrounded by angels of the Father, bringing an end to the world? If one is honest with oneself, the answer is again obvious.

What Bultmann says, therefore, is that the time has come for relentless honesty to be practiced. We really do not believe these things ourselves. No one does. Not even the most fundamentalistic in our group. So why do we not accept this fact and live with it? When we do not accept that fact, says Bultmann, we are alienating our audience, separating ourselves from those whom we really wish to reach. We are making as the standards of orthodoxy statements we really do not accept in fact. We are telling the person outside the church that to join our ranks is to subscribe to beliefs that we ourselves do not live by. As a result, the world outside the church comes to one of two conclusions. The world decides that (1) either we are hypocrites, proclaiming a theory that we reject in fact, or (2) we are idiots, embracing a world view that is as dated as the belief that the world is flat. In either event, we lose our audience; we alienate the world.

The answer, says Bultmann, is to demythologize — to make our message more relevant and palatable to the outside world. We must do this or we will die. We must take these basic factors which the New Testament holds to be central and we must reinterpret them in new thought patterns that make sense to our scientific age.

And then Bultmann goes on to show us how we must reinterpret. Yes, by all means, let us speak of demons, but let us see them, not as external concrete forces outside of us and acting upon us, but instead, as our own evil impulses, our own wrongly directed passions. These demons are to be understood, not metaphysically, but existentially, in terms of our own existence and will, as forces within us and not outside of us. Let us speak of the id, the Oedipus complex, compulsive delinquency, or terms like that, and *then* modern man will see that we are speaking to problems that he faces and that the church does have a meaning for our day.

Let us also speak of the last hour — but not as the last hour in time, that final hour lying off on the rim of the future when the whole world will collapse in flames to the sound of trumpets. No schoolboy believes that. Instead, let us speak of the last hour as the crucial hour, the critical hour, the moment of confrontation that determines a man's destiny. Let us talk of eschatology, not as a future time, but as the time when one meets Jesus. We meet him, not at the banks of the Jordan with chariots swinging low, but we meet him right now, right here, in the preaching of the church. *That* is the hour of decision, the eschatological moment when the future is forged. Eschatology must be reinterpreted, not in chronological terms, but in existential terms — the hour of decision for or against Jesus is the last hour. And again, modern man can comprehend this.

When we have done that, says Bultmann, we have demythologized. We have stripped away the archaic language of a past day and put the same message into contemporary terms.

Now at this point it becomes exceedingly important to differentiate between Bultmann's intentions and the result of those intentions. It is extremely important to see the difference between Bultmann's claims and the actual results of his program. I believe that his intention is not to destroy or pervert the gospel, but instead, to make the gospel more relevant, more vital, more significant to our time. That is his goal, to strip away the extraneous factors and to lay bare the basic nature of the Christian message. His claim is that what he is doing is simply altering the *form* of the gospel, not its *content*. He claims that we have the same unaltered story, but we now have it in a new dress. To use a word picture, what he is doing is comparing the gospel to an orange. He says that what he has done is to strip away the rind, the outer covering, the garbage that is needless, and he has laid bare the real flesh or pulp of the gospel story. He has helped the gospel rather than hindering it, for he has stripped off the encrustations, the rind, the obscuring outer shell. Or, another word picture, his claim is that he has taken the old lady and put her into a new and more attractive dress. He has made her more appealing. He has altered, not the content, only the form.

That is his intention and his claim. But I would argue that although his claim is good, the actual results are quite another thing. I would argue that he has altered not only the form but the content as well. I would argue that he has not simply put the old lady into a new dress — he has disrobed her, ravaged her, violated her. Or, to go back to the other word picture, it is not an orange he has peeled, but an onion. We all know the story of Peer Gynt and the onion. Ibsen shows Peer peeling the onion, lifting off layer after layer in seeking the core. And when he has finished peeling off the outer layers, the core is gone! The core was itself the covering. When he finished stripping away, he had nothing left. This is what Bultmann has done. He has destroyed the content, not just changed the form. He leaves us with nothing. That which comes out of the demythologizing process is not a liberating gospel, or a liberated gospel, but no gospel, no good news at all! When he has finished, there is nothing even slightly resembling the robust Christian affirmation of the New Testament.

At every single point of any consequence — the way in which Bultmann understands man, sin, the Spirit, salvation, Christ, the

A Study in Demythologizing

cross, the resurrection — the conclusions to which Bultmann comes stand in direct opposition to the views to which a person comes when he takes seriously the New Testament views of eschatology and demonology. It is not that Bultmann has rejected Satan, it is instead that he has rejected the New Testament's doctrine of man, of sin, and of grace. He ends up, not with *theo*logy, but with *anthro*pology, a man-centered study totally opposed to and differently oriented from New Testament thought.[5]

I have argued that Paul sees man as basically non-free. Man is lost, asleep in a burning room, a slave, being consumed and not even knowing it. The statistics show this to be Paul's primary view. But if one strips away Satan, one ends up with an entirely different view of man. One says, in effect, that man is not interefered with by supernatural powers outside himself. One says that man is a self-contained unit, responsible for decision, determining his own fate and destiny by his own actions. One concedes that man is exposed to factors outside his own personality, but in no case is man's attitude or action determined by those factors. That is, man is highly conditioned, and yet he is ultimately independent. And that is precisely what Bultmann is claiming: "*Man is essentially a unity*. He bears the sole responsibility for his own feeling, thinking, and willing. He is not, as the New Testament regards him, the victim of a strange dichotomy which exposes him to the interference of powers outside himself."[6] It must be noted how Bultmann himself acknowledges that this view of man is in direct opposition to the New Testament: "He is not, as the New Testament regards him . . ." It is for this reason that Bultmann could never accept the objec-

---

[5] As evidence of this, one has but to glance at the table of chapter headings on Paul that are man-centered, "Man Prior to the Revelation of Faith" and "Man Under Faith" — an entirely different approach from that of historical New Testament study, which begins with *God*.

[6] *Kerygma and Myth* (London: S.P.C.K., 1953), p. 6.

tive interpretation of Paul's conversion that we gave above, for that would show that man *is* open to the interference of powers outside himself,[7] the work of the Holy Spirit. Bultmann goes on: " Although biology and psychology recognize that man is a highly dependent being, that does not mean that he has been handed over to powers outside of himself and distinct from himself." [8] Bultmann would have to reject the Gospel stories of Jesus exorcising the demons and cleansing the demoniacs, rejecting those stories, not because they are miraculous and therefore naïve, but rejecting them instead because he does not accept their anthropology. He does not believe that man can be seized against his will by forces distinct from man. Bultmann finds himself in direct opposition to Jesus at this point. Jesus, the texts say, had compassion on those people, seeing them, not as supremely evil, having sold themselves to evil forces, having given in to evil impulses, but Jesus had compassion, seeing them as victims of frightful powers too great to resist, powers from which those victims needed liberation. Bultmann says that such a view of man is unacceptable. Man is not open to such powers.

This view of man has enormous significance, at which we have already hinted. For one will note, if he is theologically alert, that this view not only rejects Satan but it rejects the Holy Spirit as well. The Spirit and Satan are parts of the same world view, parts of the same view of man. If one says that man is not open to evil external powers, then, to be consistent, one must go on to say that man is not open to good external powers. And Bultmann is consistent. On the very same page in which he defines man and thus rejects Satan, he goes on to maintain that modern man cannot accept the doctrine of the Spirit either. " [Modern man] finds *what the New Testament has to say about the Spirit (pneuma) and the sacraments utterly strange and incomprehensible.*" [9] And thus, in the same work, in response to his critics,

[7] See above, p. 44.   [8] *Kerygma and Myth,* p. 6.   [9] *Ibid.*

Bultmann goes on to show how we can demythologize the Spirit, refusing to see it as a supernatural force interfering with man.[10] We have consistently seen how Paul places the Holy Spirit at the very center of his thought. It is the Spirit who forms our prayers, pours love into us, energizes and activates us, and brings forth all the Christian virtues.[11] At this fundamental point Bultmann places himself in direct opposition to the New Testament message: he has not altered simply the form, but he has violated the essential content.

Again, those who read carefully will have noted that in the very same sentence in which he rejected the Holy Spirit, Bultmann threw out the Sacraments as well. Again he was consistent, for the interpretation that we gave to Baptism will be remembered.[12] Baptism is God in action, seizing helpless man. That view is based on demonology. Man had to be seized because by himself he is lost. The sacramental view is based upon and demands demonology. Without a view that accepts Satan as a real force, holding man helpless, the Sacraments become incomprehensible.[13] This Bultmann sees, and hence he dismisses the Sacraments.

Or, to move in another direction. We have seen that the key-

[10] *Ibid.*, p. 22. He writes: "The Spirit does not work like a supernatural force, nor is it the permanent possession of the believer. It is the possibility of a new life which must be appropriated by deliberate resolve. . . . Thus the 'Spirit' concept has been emancipated from mythology." And again he writes: "Modern man . . . is undoubtedly right in regarding his ego in its subjective aspects as a unity, and in refusing to allow any room for alien powers to interfere with his subjective life. The mythical thought of the New Testament . . . does reckon with such interferences" (p. 120).

[11] See above, pp. 104–106.

[12] See above, pp. 101–103.

[13] For example, Anabaptist groups see sin as rebellion, not bondage. This is why they have altar calls, revival meetings, replete with pleas for repentance. It is no coincidence that the Anabaptist group consequently does not see Baptism as a true sacrament, an act of God. Hence, there is no infant Baptism in their circles.

stone of Paul's thought was the fact of the resurrection — the literal historical fact of a true corporal resurrection.[14] If that fact were not true, all of Christianity was a lie. But that stress was possible in Paul only because he saw the resurrection as a victory over the devil. (Here Heb. 2:14 reflects the early Christian belief that the only reason Jesus even became incarnate at all was to enter into death and thus destroy the devil who had the power of death, " He himself likewise partook of the same nature, that through death he might destroy him who has the power of death, that is, the devil.") Death was a weapon of Satan, the last great weapon or enemy; thus victory here was victory indeed — vital proof of the superiority of Jesus, the rock upon which the hope of the church rested. But if one rejects Satan, the resurrection loses all vitality and significance, and it can be rejected. And reject it Bultmann does: " An historical event which includes resurrection from the dead is utterly inconceivable."[15] As shocking as the phrase may be for pious ears, it is absolutely consistent with his point of view — and consistent, unfortunately, with most of contemporary theology.[16] If the work of Jesus is

[14] See above, pp. 78–79.

[15] Bultmann goes on to say: "If the event of Easter day is in any sense an historical event additional to the event of the cross, it is nothing else than the rise of faith in the risen Lord. . . . The resurrection itself is not an event of past history " (*Kerygma and Myth,* pp. 39, 42).

[16] Klausner, a Jew, is sympathetic in his treatment of the Christian message — until he speaks of the resurrection! For he knows that if he concedes the truth of that event, he has conceded too much. And therefore, Klausner attacks the resurrection with a vehemence seen nowhere else in his commentaries on the Christian message. In *From Jesus to Paul,* he seeks to discredit the resurrection accounts by calling into question the reliability of the witnesses: " Mary Magdalene . . . hysterical to the point of madness. . . . The women and the disciples actually saw Jesus . . . in a vision which appeared to them, enthusiastic to the point of madness and credulous to the point of blindness. . . . Peter also saw Jesus . . . incurably emotional and visionary, he had already seen strange visions at Caesarea Philippi " (pp. 255–256, 265). It is disconcerting to see this same attempt to reduce the resurrection to an emotional hallucination, entirely

purely existential, overcoming our bad impulses, then objective events and victories such as exorcisms of demons and resurrection from the dead lose all importance and can be minimized and rejected.[17]

Or, again, to move in still another direction, we have already seen that the Satanward view demands that we see Jesus as divine. Only a divine figure sent of God could stand up to so mighty a foe as Satan.[18] The divinity of Jesus was not a fabrication of the church. It was a claim of Jesus himself. He had to be divine in order to meet the foe. And Paul developed his Christology in respect to the evil forces. The growth of enemy opposition was what forced Paul to spell out clearly the divinity of Jesus.[19] Thus, if one rejects Satan, the divinity of Jesus becomes incomprehensible and absurd. Hence Bultmann, radically and ruthlessly consistent, writes: " What a primitive mythology it is, that a divine Being should become incarnate, and atone for the sins of men through his own blood."[20] The sentence needs

---

understandable in non-Christian writings, repeated in Christian works. See, for example, Rudolf Otto, *The Kingdom of God and the Son of Man* (London: Lutterworth Press, 1951), p. 374, where he reduces the resurrection to a hallucinatory result of intense yearning. For the early church, resurrection faith depended upon the resurrection (the Emmaus story, Luke 24:13 f.); contemporary theology would reverse this (Denney too, because of his demythologizing, has no place for the resurrection — see Ch. 2, n. 2, above.)

[17] This we take to be the meaning of Edwin C. Hoskyns and F. Noel Davey when they write: " When once the center and authority of religion is found not in the action or revelation of God, in the person of the man Jesus, but in the spiritual experience of those who claim to know Jesus in their hearts, the historical life of Jesus is relegated to a secondary part of religion, and ceases to be a necessary dynamic part of religion " (*The Riddle of the New Testament*, p. 151; London: Faber & Faber, Ltd., 1952).

[18] Aulén (to whose writings I owe much) insists: " Christ came down from heaven because no other power than that of God himself was able to accomplish the work that was to be done." (*Christus Victor*, p. 32).

[19] See above, pp. 127–130.

[20] *Kerygma and Myth*, p. 7.

no rebuttal. It is not Christian.

We have already seen Bultmann's view of the Holy Spirit. The implications of that view for a Christian view of the Trinity are self-evident and enormous. Yet, as enormous as they are, he undermines the Christian view of the Trinity from still another route. Bultmann has a Greek or a scientific view of God. Let me explain. When Darwinism and the first theories of evolution were put forth, the church was alarmed and resisted, but then we made peace, insisting that there was no conflict between religion and science. Now, as far as the Creation story itself is concerned, that is true. There is no conflict. Whether the world was made immediately, as Genesis seems to suggest, or whether it was made mediately, in a long process, as evolution seems to suggest, there is no difference, for it does not alter the basic Biblical claim that God was the power behind the process, no matter what the process may have been. The Apostles' Creed does not say how God created the heavens and the earth; it does not give a doctrine of creation. It instead gives a doctrine of the Creator. There is no point of conflict.

Yet, to go on from there and say that no conflict between religion and science exists is to be naïve and unrealistic. There is a conflict. Greek scientific thought had a clearly defined view of God. Greek scientific thought held that God acted according to the use of clearly defined rules and principles. If one could determine through the use of reason what these rules were, one could build upon those principles, adapt one's environment, and control one's destiny. That is why Hellenism began with such an affirmative view of man. Put in simplest terms, the Greeks believed that if one performed the same experiment seven times and always got the same results, one could perform the same experiment seven hundred more times and always, if the circumstances were the same, the results would be the same. The Greeks had a detached view of God, a God who worked by the rules. That God did not

A Study in Demythologizing

plunge into the cosmos unpredictably, altering all the rules, bringing forth unexpected results. This is why the Greeks stressed, at the outset, not liberation, but education. Man had locked in his own brain the key to the universe (when the key failed to unlock, of course, and when man found that education did not improve things, the later pessimistic view of man as enslaved developed, as is seen in Sophocles' *Oedipus Rex* — but to develop this would take us too far afield). This was the assumption of the Greeks, and this is the assumption of modern Western man. This is our scientific view. It is a secularized view that leaves a living God out of all consideration. Or, if it posits a God at all, it is a God who lives by the rules and does not disrupt the normal processes. This is why the Greek was the first to practice experimental medicine and investigate the nature of rainfall. This is the Greek view, this is modern man's view, and this is Bultmann's view. This is why Bultmann can lean on modern science and summon forth biology and psychology to support him. But I would insist that this is not the Biblical view. The Bible does not show us a God who is confined by rules, whose interventions are nonexistent, and who conducts himself by standards that we can discover through the use of reason. The Bible instead argues for a living God who plunges into this world and is able to reverse all the logical conclusions of men. This God lives all through the Bible. At the exodus, by every standard of evaluation of political science, the Jews were under the heel of the mightiest temporal power of the day, Pharaoh, and there was no chance of rescue. And yet they were rescued. In Hezekiah's time, by every standard of the science of logistics and military logic, Jerusalem was doomed before the troops of Sennacherib and would not survive. It did survive. The walls of Jericho came tumbling down. Paul went off on the Damascus road and was turned inside out. There is a living God who does not play by the rules. There is a powerful God who is unpredictable and uncontrollable, sheer will, not harnessed by logic or laws — not arbitrary and capricious, but supreme, omnipotent. It is for this reason that the Jews were not a scientific people. It was Aristotle who fiddled with rainfall and experimented with corpses; the Jew could not. The Hebrew could never be a scientist because his view of God would not allow it.

What Bultmann has given us is not a Biblical God at all, but a reincarnation of Greek scientific thought. In his attempt to make the gospel more relevant to a Greek-oriented scientific thought world, he has rejected the Biblical God, capitulated to the world, lost the very core of Christian thinking, and left us with a grim graceless humanism.[21]

This is the situation in which we find ourselves today. It is for this reason that the church finds itself on the sidelines, and we hear the phrase repeated, even by eminent churchmen, that we are living in the secular age, in the post-Christian era. The church has lost all significance. The claim of Bultmann is that we must therefore adapt to survive. I would argue back that the reason we are dying is that we have already adapted. In our attempt to be relevant, we have lost that which we had to offer. This is the dilemma of our day. Bultmann tells us to demythologize or die. I would argue, we have demythologized, and that is why we are dead. He tells us, demythologize or we lose our audience. I answer, we have demythologized, gained an audience, and lost a message. We have people listening to us, but we have nothing to tell them that the secular world cannot say better.

What, then, is the answer? The answer, perhaps, is that some new form of demythologizing must be found. Perhaps demythologizing is not wrong in principle, just wrong in the routes it has

[21] In *Eschatology and Ethics* (Harper & Row, Publishers, Inc., 1950), p. 191, Amos Wilder writes: "A further criticism of Bultmann would demur, finally, at the absence in his total picture of the feature of grace, the positive aspect of the gospel . . . utterly grim and stern aspect of the whole Bultmann picture."

A Study in Demythologizing

thus far taken. Perhaps we must continue to demythologize, along different lines, until we can be sure that it is only the form and not the content that we alter. This is a possible answer to the dilemma. But I would argue on other terms.

I would argue that Bultmann has sold us a bill of goods. I would argue that no demythologizing is necessary. I would argue that whereas Bultmann finds demonology repulsive and inexplicable, perhaps modern man does not. Bultmann, who claims to represent modern man, does not represent modern man at all. Bultmann's thought patterns were calcified fifty years ago. His creative work was done in a generation long passed away, and he does not know the man of our day. Bultmann is an old man now, out of touch with reality. He expresses a view of man that was popular before the First World War, when we had an optimistic and affirmative evaluation of man. Before the First World War, there was a positive view of man, the belief that through education man could achieve Utopia on earth. It was felt, then, that progress was automatic. Darwinism had become a philosophy, and every day in every way things were getting better all the time. Man had not fallen. Instead he had begun on his knees, was now climbing upward, and given enough time, would leave the slime of the swamp behind him and evolutionary processes would produce the Ideal Man in the Ideal Society. But the old Y.M.C.A. morality — build enough swimming pools and get rid of sin, adjust the environment and enlighten man and you can redeem him — that view in our day is dead. Two world wars sandwiched around an economic depression, followed by another war, the Korean, to which we did not assign a number, followed in its turn by the constant threat of nuclear extermination that overshadows our time, have laid to rest finally and fully the earlier naïve view of man, the optimistic view.

The world view of our time is different. It has come to see man as the New Testament sees him — man as helpless, living in an absurd world, ruled over by evil powers. But although that is the world view of our time, it is recognized as such only by the secular world and not by the church. At the very moment that Bultmann is telling us that modern man cannot accept the idea of man as helpless, living in an absurd cosmos buffeted by malignant forces, at that very moment, Jean-Paul Sartre walks across the Jardin du Luxembourg, runs into an almond tree, and says: "Absurd, absurd. . . . Who put that tree there? Who or what power seeks to disrupt me?" Things are not what they ought to be. At the same time that Bultmann speaks for the modern man and says that the devil is obsolete and out of style, Albert Camus is winning the Nobel Prize for literature for *La Peste*, telling us that this world is twisted and deformed. In the book, the doctor comes home and finds a dead rat on the steps, and ponders that that is not where dead rats belong. Something is out of joint. How out of joint is seen in what follows. The dead rat is a carrier of bubonic plague, and the whole north African town is decimated and destroyed. Man is the victim of enormous forces over which he has no control. And in the midst of the plague, Camus shows us the bankruptcy of the church. The priest stands up — and in good Godward fashion he insists that the affliction is not the work of Satan, evil powers run amuck, but instead, it is the punishment of a holy God on the sins of the people. It is a bankrupt view because the suffering is out of all proportion to man's sin. Bankrupt because, as the Jew saw in the apocalyptic period, if you make God the author of tragedy, there is no answer to tragedy, only despair. And that is why Camus and Sartre have only despair, are only apostles of pessimism. They see the problem, more clearly than Bultmann, but they have no answer, there is "no exit."[22]

At the very moment that Bultmann tells us that man is free and

[22] An allusion, of course, to Sartre's play of that title in which he seems to be saying that hell is people, and there is no way out.

A Study in Demythologizing

self-determining, modern technology and modern art and literature cry out that modern man does not see it that way. Man is no longer an individual, much less a self-determining individual. He is not even a number anymore — only a hole in an IBM card — the depth of nothingness. Modern statuary, with its deformed and grotesque figures, holes through the middle, welded out of scrap from the trash heap, all cry out that we have no concept of modern man that is positive and affirmative. The muddled, confused trivia of Picasso, with a breast looming out of a forehead, an arm growing out of an ear, tells us that no longer can we identify man. The literature of our day, all the poor Willie Lomans who do not know who they are, shows us modern man as lost in his skyscraper cliffs and asphalt jungles, lost in the maze of electric wires and manufactured recreation.

The answer is the Satanward view — a healthy recognition of the tragic perversion of life as it was intended to be. But above the recognition, there is the cry of liberation, the insistence that God is not the source of anguish, the cause of despair, but is instead the answer, the rescuing one, the liberating Redeemer who has acted once and who will act again. We openly recognize the malignancy of the world in which we find ourselves. We recognize the fearful sense of helplessness that dominates modern man and makes him cower in packs and organizations. But we cry out against those fears and insist that the hopes and fears of all the years were met in Bethlehem, mastered in the resurrection, and shall be soothed away at the return when every eye shall be wiped dry and there will be weeping no more.

Bultmann has sold us a bill of goods. A future generation, looking at our impoverished exclusively Godward view of Christianity, will ask how we were able to survive on such meager fare. The answer to our problem is not to adapt to society's despairing view, but to lift man up to a higher vision. It is they, outside the church, not we, who must change. The answer is to be found, not in new techniques, in new insights of chemistry and psychiatry, but in a return to the principles of the Reformers. They cried out loud and clear that "we are by nature sinful and unclean" and that "I believe by my own reason or strength I cannot believe." But they also preached a conquering Christ, an empty cross — the symbol of the Reformers was not an eternally suffering Jesus nailed to a cross bar, but an empty cross! A risen Lord, a triumphant Redeemer! Therefore their hymns abounded with a strident note of victory within warfare. "A Mighty Fortress Is Our God," wrote Luther. It is true, as he says in stanza one, that on earth is not his equal — Satan rules supreme. But Luther does not end with stanza one, with Satan ruling. He goes on to insist that the Man of God's own choosing will overthrow him.

The Satanward view was once, in the vibrant golden age of Protestantism, the central view. It is not now, and that is why we are crippled.

www.ingramcontent.com/pod-product-compliance
Lightning Source LLC
Chambersburg PA
CBHW050826160426
43192CB00010B/1915